They're all foreigners abroad!

They're all foreigners abroad!

Hilarious A - Z of Brits on Holiday

Stuart Wright

PNEUMA SPRINGS PUBLISHING UK

First Published in 2009 by:
Pneuma Springs Publishing

They're all foreigners abroad
Copyright © 2009   Stuart Wright
ISBN: 978-1-905809-63-9

Pneuma Springs Publisl ing
A Subsidiary of Pneuma
7 Groveherst Road, Dar
E: admin@pneumaspring
W: www.pneumaspring

A catalogue record for this book is available from the British Library.

This book is for my wife Chris, my son Oliver, his wife Katie and my step children Justine and Jonathan

INTRODUCTION

Why do the Brits have such a bad reputation whilst on their holidays abroad?

What is it about us that makes us stand out from other tourists? We are a strange nation, but I don't think that we're much different to everyone else, apart from maybe the alcohol consumption. You don't have to be British in order to wear socks with sandals and you certainly don't have to be British in order to be a bigot, a slob or a snob. Stereotyping can be dangerous, but I guess we all do it from time to time and let's be honest; we Brits are not difficult to take the mickey out of whilst on our hard earned holidays.

You never know, you may recognize yourself; I would be surprised if you don't. If the cap fits, wear it. It could be me, it could be you, and it could be him or her over there? If you say that you don't recognize yourself within this book then quite frankly, I don't believe you. Go on, have a laugh at yourself. We're all guilty of being petty and stupid in one way or another, especially on holiday!

If you haven't done it then you've seen it, and if you haven't seen it then you've thought it. You won't have to look very far for yourself in this book!

Before we begin, I make no apology whatsoever for starting this A to Z book with the letter H (HRT actually). It has nothing at all to do with the schools I attended, as I know the alphabet really begins with the letter A. This one deliberate mistake on my part could save the lives of many middle aged men. If you read on, I'm sure you'll agree that the letter H is king in the holiday preparation stakes:–

HRT (hormone replacement tablets)

They're important, very important indeed, more important than your suitcase, more important than anything you could ever think of. If your wife forgets them, then you're dead on your hard earned holiday. You may wake up with a bread knife stuck in you one morning or you may not wake up at all. I say this from a blokey perspective, its self preservation really. I want to live a lot longer and I guess you do too, but you won't if your wife or partner forgets the old HRTs. If that happens, you're wasted!

Come on ladies, I know us guys are not very good at packing but come on, do us both a favour. Check the obvious 'passports, money, airline tickets'. Then, PLEASE, make sure that you have packed your HRT tablets – PLEASE!

I have had personal experience of the 'no HRT lady' and it really is poo your pants frightening! It can start with a frosty look; going all quiet on you; tutting; rolling the eyes in that 'What the hell are you on about' look; going out of their way to bump into you as if you are an obstruction when you are actually standing at least a yard away from them and they also accuse you of moving something about which you know absolutely nothing. I could go on, but the upshot is that you/me (man) is a proper tosser and not worth the time of day.

I wouldn't mind, but I haven't done anything wrong on my holiday – yet!

A

A bargain holiday

Mr. and Mrs. 'We got a real bargain holiday' get right up my nostrils. Within a few hours of arriving at your hotel, I can almost guarantee that a couple will verbally force themselves upon you because they are dying to ask you how much you paid for your holiday. The reason for this is that they waited until the very last minute before booking theirs over the Internet or on Teletext. It's as if they go out of their way to really naff you off. You paid over a thousand pounds for your two weeks holiday in the four star hotel, but they can't wait to tell everyone that they only paid three hundred and fifty pounds. When they landed at the airport they didn't have a clue which hotel they would get, but they struck lucky and got your very nice four star.

Never mind; there's always next year and let's hope they get put into a dustbin!

A couple of beers

Why is it that when a man says to his wife on holiday – 'I'm just going for a couple of beers', the lady thinks the man actually means TWO beers? We don't mean it; it's just a figure of speech ladies. When we say 'A couple of beers,' what we actually mean is loads and loads of beers! Can we just sort this one out straight away in order for there to be no misunderstandings during the holiday? It's no different really from a lady saying 'I'm just going to have a wander around the shops for ten minutes'. What that really means is two hours - at least!

You see, you ladies are no better than us men when it comes to doing the things you want to do but daren't say it properly!

Accents

Now here's a funny thing. When you are within your own surroundings in the UK your accent means nothing at all because everyone around you speaks the same way. When you go on holiday however, you are mixing with people from every different corner of the UK. They sound completely different to you. On the other hand, you sound completely different to them. You're not amongst your own now and you probably sound totally stupid to most of your fellow holiday makers.

If you have a strong accent you won't realize it, but just observe some of the looks you get from other holiday makers. You will also get people saying 'No' to you when you expected them to say 'Yes', and vice versa. The reason for this is that the person concerned won't have a clue what you're talking about and rather than asking you to repeat the question for a sixth time, they will play safe. Yes or no? They know they have a fifty fifty chance of getting it right and just take a stab, 'Er, er - - - Yes'. You then give them a confused look and all they now have to say is 'I mean no'. You are now happy that they have answered you correctly but for all they know, you could have been asking if chocolate is made from grass!

Yorkshire person	*'Good ere int it'?*
Liverpool person	*'Ar right la'*
Welsh person	*'Llan goch googoo goch – Tom Jones'*
North Lancashire person	*'Av yer gor a drink av yer not'*
Geordie person	*'Wai ai man'*
Brummie person	*'Tara a bit'*
Scottish person	*'Och ay the noo an see yu Jimmy'*
Surrey person	*'Oh hello, so charming to meet you'* - what's he on about?

You sound stupid to most other people. Admit it!

Adjusting ones self (men)

Anywhere in the world you care to name, men will be seen adjusting themselves whilst walking down the street. On holiday, however, for some strange reason this occupation is far more evident. Is it because men are not used to wearing shorts, is it the heat, or is it just that they are genuinely excited because they're on holiday? If there is a party of men walking down a street or along the promenade, it sometimes appears that they are playing synchronized pocket billiards. They often don't appear to be anything like embarrassed or self conscious about these movements and indeed some of them appear to be quite proud.

It's not right is it?

Advice to new arrivals

If you are on a two week holiday then the chances are that new arrivals will get talking to you at the beginning of your second week. You have already been there for a week and they want to know the score. The best thing to do is just ignore them because you must have done it at some point in the past and then wished to hell that you hadn't bothered.

'Oh yes, we've tried quite a few of the restaurants and the best we have found is the Miramar. The food is excellent and the service is spot on.'

The next day you see these people again and you can tell by their faces what's coming next.

'We took your advice and went to the Miramar last night. It was awful! The waiter was ignorant, the food was cold, and I'm sure the soup starter was packet soup.'

'Oh, er, the Miramar? We haven't been there. We said the Viramar. Yes, the Viramar, it really is very good there but we can't remember where it is'.

Liar!

Aeros

Bubbly chocolate bars. After your first few hours in a Eurozone country, don't rush down to the nearest sweet shop for thirty Aero bars. Aeros are not really the currency in mainland Europe. On your first visit to a Euro shop, café or restaurant you will be forgiven for thinking that you should be paying the bill in bubbly chocolate bars. You see, many Eurozoners do not pronounce the word euro as we do 'Euro', they pronounce it 'Aero'. Just for a laugh, when you're asked for five aeros for your drinks, just say to the waiter 'Certainly, peppermint, orange or milk chocolate' and then give him the melted ones in your shorts pocket.

I'm sure he'll see the funny side of it?

After shave and perfume counterfeits

There are shops, market stalls and guys in shabby clothes all over foreign holiday resorts selling counterfeit after shaves and perfumes. You can buy all of your favourite fragrances for a fraction of the proper price. The packaging is excellent and you wouldn't know the difference from the real thing. Once you open the carton and smell the stuff, you are more than pleasantly surprised that it actually smells the same as the original one does. Only for about three and a half seconds though - then it's gone!

Whatever you do, don't give one of these counterfeit after shaves or perfumes to a friend or relative who either smokes, has a real fire or an Aga cooker. If you do, then you are on a manslaughter charge. There is so much spirit in this stuff that if you strike a match near your face once applied then you are toasted, fried, on fire, gone up in smoke.

You may as well put lighter fluid on your face. Come to think of it, you probably are!

Aircraft seats (yours)

Which row are you in?

Doesn't it really annoy you when you get put in row number 14?

You leg it to the departure gate once the flight goes on screen and then wait for about two weeks before boarding commences. Everyone is jousting for position as near to the front as possible and then the call comes – 'Could all passengers sitting in rows 15 to 30 please board the plane first.'

You're in row 14 – Aaaaaaaargh, that's not fair!

Aircraft toilets

Have you ever wondered when you go to the toilet on a plane where all the wotsit goes?

I always assumed that it went into some kind of holding tank which was then emptied at the next airport. Then – someone told me that it goes straight outside at tremendous force and that due to the altitude, the wee wee and wotsit is immediately vaporized. Is that right? I find it difficult to believe that with all the thousands of flights every day there wouldn't be stuff falling out of the sky all over the world and yet I've never seen any. I sometimes wonder if dogs are misunderstood. Is it possible that the dog poo on the pavement outside your front gate may not be dog poo at all? It might have fallen out of a plane during the night.

What do you think?

Airport bars

Are they a rip off or what?

You can spend half of your holiday spending money in the airport bar. Where on earth do they get those prices from? It's no wonder that half of the people in airport bars are sneaking their own (home filled) miniatures into a mixer. Just have a look next time you're in the airport bar. 'Just one coke and one tonic water please'. At that point, start watching them out of the corner of your eye. They sit down and then scan the area before reaching into their bag or pocket for the miniature Bacardi and miniature Gin.

At those prices who can blame me? I mean them!

Airport security

Due to recent terrorist activities, airport security is far stricter than it used to be. People complain about being held up or having to take their shoes off, which is a bit unreasonable really as it's far better to be slightly delayed than finish up in pieces at the bottom of the ocean. Having said that, certain 'Diligent Dons' within airport security appear to enjoy a little over the top activity. A friend of mine recently had personal experience of 'Diligent Don' at a UK airport and this is a perfectly true story:

Everyone has a favourite food and mine is Gala pie. I would risk prison for a slice of that beautiful pork pie with boiled eggs running through the middle of it but it's like gold dust abroad. Recently, some friends of ours (Martin and Kim) were coming over to their apartment in Mijas Costa so as a treat; he said he would bring me a full Gala pie – wow – yum yum! He went to great lengths in order for me to prolong the enjoyment of this great treat. Kim went to see the manager at the deli' counter of their local supermarket and explained the situation. She ordered a huge full pie, fully sealed, ingredients listed and with the longest 'Best before' date possible – sorted! Just prior to their departure for the airport, my Gala pie was collected and off they go with the standard issue two suitcases and a pie resembling a breeze block as hand luggage. As they were going through the scanner one of the security type people asked Martin to open the bag containing my gala pie and said:

'What's that?'

'Gala pie for my friend Stuart in Spain – he loves it and I'm dying to see his face when he sees the size of that thing.'

'You can't take it' said the man with a huge grin on his face and slavering at the thought of his new found lunch.

'What do you mean I can't take it; I ordered it specially – it's sealed, it has an ingredients list and I even have the telephone number of the deli' manager who you can call to confirm it's okay.'

'No – more than my jobs worth is that. The pie stays here with me' – slaver slaver.'

13

Now Martin is a nice guy but when he loses it he's like a nuclear warhead that swears a lot. I obviously wasn't actually there at the time, but when he explained the proceedings to me, I was nearly wetting myself laughing –

'You want this for your own lunch don't you?'

'No – just following procedures,' he said with a snigger.

'Do you really think I have an exploding gala pie?'

'Just doing my job sir – snigger snigger, slaver slaver.'

Oh no – Martin's lost it now!

'Right, that's it you plank. Look at him; yes that bloke who's just walked straight past you. Is that a gun in his pocket or is he just over excited because he's going on holiday? What about her over there with the big stupid springy bouncy trainers on – they look as though they could explode to me'.

'Now now sir – it's only a pie – slaver slaver.'

'Only a pie, only a ******* pie – it's a Gala pie and it's for my mate who loves them and you want it for yourself don't you - well watch this then.'

At this point Martin lost the plot completely. He lifted this gastronomic delight above his head and smashed it to the floor. He then proceeded to jump up and down on it until the wrapper fractured and the pie exploded all over Diligent Don's lovely shiny floor. 'If my mate Stuart can't eat it, then as sure as hell you can't mate.'

Martin had to be restrained and after a serious amount of cooling down and apologizing they did eventually let him board the plane.

Airport security – it can make you lose your temper!

Air stewards (male cabin crew)

It's wrong to stereotype people – but. Yes, you know what I'm going to say don't you?

I am absolutely convinced that there must be a few blokey type air stewards but I've never seen one. What is it about a cabin crew job that attracts these guys? Did they think they would get to wear a skirt and a hair ribbon when they applied? They're nice, very nice, and a bit too nice really. I am not trying to say for one minute that they're all fully paid up Trannie's, but you do have to wonder don't you? They mince around with a limp wrist and act all girly.

You can imagine if they didn't have that trolley that they would skip down the aisle shouting 'Tea, coffee – extra's?'

Alarm clocks

You shouldn't need your alarm clock on holiday if you are going to relax, but people take them don't they? I bet you take your mobile telephone. There's an alarm clock on that; well, most of them anyway. The problem is that if you're over forty years old then you haven't got a clue how to work the alarm clock on your mobile telephone. If you learnt, then it would save you from taking your big daft one! Also, on most mobile phones there is a calculator, but you don't know how that works either, so you take a calculator as well.

Learn how to operate your mobile phone properly and stop paying excess baggage for all the things you don't need. You're still on gas!

Always wrong!

If you get into an argument with a foreigner in their own country, or worse still, if you finish up having a proper fight with a foreigner – you're wrong! Remember, in other countries they look after their own. You could have an altercation with a foreigner and when the police turn up you have a hatchet in your head whilst the local only has a lip stick kiss mark on his cheek, but it's your fault! Whatever the circumstances are, it is you (the Brit) who is guilty until found innocent, whilst the local is innocent until found guilty. That's the way it is abroad. It's the opposite of the UK.

They look after their own abroad you know!

Amazingly silly soldiers

Now here's a very strange thing! Why is it that whichever country you visit on holiday they all appear to have amazingly silly soldiers? They usually reside at the country's capital city and it appears to me that there is some kind of global competition going on in order to see who can have the silliest soldiers.

We don't do too badly ourselves in the silly soldier stakes. We have the Beefeaters and they don't come looking a lot sillier than that.

What about the Swiss Guards at the Vatican City in Rome? Phhhhhhooooooaaaaaa, chuckle, chuckle! Brightly coloured stripey girly dress type thingies with brightly coloured stripey stockings holding a long stick with a piece of metal on the end of it. Now; let's just say that some loony terrorist type people wanted to attack the Vatican. Out of a white Transit van they would jump with machine guns, hand grenades, smoke bombs and the lot. Up to the Vatican they would run, bobbing and weaving through the large pillars and porticos until they got to the sentry boxes where they would see their enemy 'The Swiss Guards'. You can just picture it now can't you?

'Ha ha ha ha; pheeeeeeeew, oh my, you're having a laugh aren't you? Heeeeeeee, who the hell are you then?' The terrorists are doubled up laughing now and peeing their pants. 'Oh Christ; you can't be serious. I can't shoot you because you're a girly. They didn't tell me that I would have to fight a shop window manikin who looks like a stick of rock. Pheeeeeeew, look, I've wet myself now. Oh I can't stand this any more, I'm going home.'

What about the Greek Presidential Guards? Now they really are side slapping funny. They wear a three quarter length frock coat type thingy held tightly around the waist by a black leather belt.

They then wear tights (or they could be stockings and suspenders) with a cord around both knees and a tassle hanging off it behind the knees. It's a bit like a ponsy shin pad in reverse-ish! They also have these humungously long shoes, the design of which must come from Charlie Corroley or some such clown. To top the shoes off, they have a big pom pom stuck to the end of the toe; the reason for which I have absolutely no idea. They then have a hat which looks like an upside down milk pan with a tassle hanging from it. How much do these guys get paid? It may just be me, but I would have to be paid an absolute fortune to get dressed up like they do. As if the uniform isn't bad enough; have you seen their walk? They kick their legs out in front of them like they are desperately trying to break wind or something. It's just not right!

Don't send the same terrorist type person to Greece or he will surely finish up in a lunatic asylum. He'll think that his terrorist boss is taking the mickey out of him.

Then we have the guard at the Royal Palace in Monte Carlo who looks (a bit) like a British Bobby who can't dress himself properly. He has a fairly standard navy blue Bobby type suit on, spats over his boots, loads of ribbons on his lapel and then a Bobby type helmet which looks as if he has just got it out of a Christmas cracker – phwoooooaagh, chuckle, chuckle!

Silly soldiers! They're only having a laugh aren't they?

Would they frighten you? I don't think so!

Ants

In hot countries there are ten trillion, billion, squillion ants on every square metre of land. I just made that up, but there are a lot of them. Where do they all come from and where do they all go to once they've nicked the crumbs from your sandwiches? I find it fascinating watching these little things marching in regimented lines, carrying off their booty to some unknown place which must be incredibly overcrowded and smelly. When I watch them, they remind me of when I visit England. Everybody is running around all the time. The only difference is that most people in England don't pinch the crumbs from your sandwiches.

Come to think of it, they pinch your car or your TV instead!

Arrival at your hotel

You leg it don't you – from the coach to the hotel reception. Why? You think that if you get to the reception desk first then you will get the best room. Not true! The hotel rooms have already been allocated before you even get there, so what's the rush. You should look around you at other tourists who were on the same coach as you. Inevitably you will see a middle aged to elderly couple sat in the corner of reception with a gin and tonic in their hands sniggering at you. What's the rush? Their room was allocated to them before they even got off the plane and so was yours. You're here to relax, what's wrong with you? You will get exactly the same room if you are at the front of the queue as you would if you were at the back of the queue. Look at you, all stressed out. Look at them, a gin and tonic and all's well, same rooms.

Who's got it wrong? You have.

Arthritis

Many people in the UK suffer from arthritis and yet whilst they are on holiday abroad they don't suffer with pain or stiffness at all. We have met lots of UK sufferers who are completely and utterly pain free once they arrive at their sunny holiday destination. So, to all arthritis sufferers, that's another reason why you should go on holiday to the sun.

The only thing you might get is an arthritic willy, but that's not a bad swap is it?

Artists (pi*s)

Are you one of them?

You will see drunken foreigners abroad, but not many. They're mostly British! As for you; yes you. I bet you're one of those self righteous tourists who look at legless Brits and say things like, 'Look at him, he's drunk. It's people like him who give us Brits a bad name'. Then, a couple of nights later, you have a few drinks and then a few more; you then down a cocktail or ten. Yes, now you look like that guy did a few nights ago. It's you; you're as bad as him aren't you? But that's different isn't it? No! You're the alci now - old giggly knickers. Other Brits are saying exactly the same things about you as you did the other night about him.

Who's right and who's wrong eh?

Artists (sand)

These people are very clever; I think so anyway. You can walk along the sea front in many foreign holiday resorts and see these huge sand sculptures on the beach. They can make crocodiles, dolphins, you name it and these people can sculpture them in sand. Fantastic and very clever, but hardly anyone gives them any money. The reason for this is that these people are on the beach next to their sculpture a few metres away from you and therefore, not intimidating. It's not fair really if you think about it. You will be eating a meal or having a drink in a bar when some atrocious musician comes in and because he's in your face with a begging bowl, you will give him some money. Yet this sand sculpture artist person gets zilch and he's the talented one. It could be me, but I have seen supposed art on the TV which looks like a couple of old prams welded together and then there was once a pickled cow or something in a glass jar. I don't know about artists, con artists maybe.

Sand art – that's proper talent. Go on, give him something. He's got far more talent than Paco the naff guitar player!

Audio language lessons in the car

Have you seen them in the UK, sat in traffic jams or waiting for the traffic lights to change? People who are obviously trying to learn the language prior to going on their holiday – ha ha, phew! They are sat there in their car, totally oblivious to everything going on outside as they are totally absorbed in their own personal foreign language lesson. They're talking away to themselves which is fair enough really, but to anyone watching them from outside their car they look like total retards. 'Por favor – gracias - hasta luego'. They're away with the fairies and already fancy themselves in a sombrero, beret or whatever.

Get your car windows tinted when you buy a language CD because you look like a proper twonker to anyone watching you.

B

Baby powder

A good use for baby powder is for yourself on the beach. If you get covered in sand then it hurts when you try to wipe it off, particularly if you have a little sun burn. Sprinkle some baby powder over the sand and then wipe very gently. All the sand just falls off with no pain whatsoever.

Bandanas

Oh boy, fat old baldy men in bandanas – chuckle chuckle! I'm going to be a bit controversial here and say that I think apart from on young children and teenagers, they look completely and utterly – er - stupid! Everybody has the right to wear whatever they like, but bandanas on fully grown men – come on!

In the bandana stakes we have – Fat belly peoples bandanas

Pensioner's bandanas

Baldy men bandanas

Baldy men with a pony tail bandanas

Just plain stupid looking bandanas

Years and years ago, some old men used to wear a knotted hanky on their head at the seaside and for some strange reason these appear to have evolved into brightly coloured bandanas. So:

which look the most stupid, knotted hankies or bandanas? Er, both actually! I can't understand why any male over the age of around eighteen would want to wear one anyway. In the hot weather, the last thing you want is a scarf stuck to your head.

Is it Kung Fu; is that it? Do they think that everyone will think they are Kung Fu experts? Yeah right, of course we will!

Is it that they were pirates in a previous life? If so, I believe they would look far less stupid with a parrot on their shoulder!

Bar and restaurant toilets

Check em out abroad! If you are only going into somewhere for a drink then I don't suppose it's all that important. If however, you are thinking of eating a meal, then just order a drink first. They say that if a place has clean toilets then the chances are that the kitchen is clean. It's true, that is a perfectly logical and true statement. There are eating houses abroad which are run by dirty people. If you cannot see into the kitchen then look at the loo's because they're a giveaway.

WARNING - Be careful though; wandering around poking your nose inside toilet doors can make other people think that you're some kind of pervert!

Bar stools

What is it about tall bar stools on holiday that makes it impossible for you to leave the place and go home? I'll tell you - embarrassment!

You can't leave because you know that you're wasted and if you try to get off that bar stool which appears to have grown two feet since you sat on it, you will make a complete plant pot of yourself. Everyone will know that you're wasted because you will wobble, fall over, knock glasses off the bar and put five people into hospital. What do you do? You order another drink, which makes you even more wasted and even more incapable of getting off the stool than you were before. It's even worse now because you're dying to go to the toilet but there is no way that you can get off the stool without making a scene. What do you do?

I'd tell you, but I can't remember!

Baseball caps (for baldies)

Baseball caps are incredibly popular with all sorts of people on holiday but be very careful if you are a baldy man (see also syrups). You might think that you are clever hiding your head skin during the day, but come the evening time you're stuck with the baseball cap pal. Why? Because you will look a bit of a wassock walking around with a body and face tan and a white head! Mind you, it won't all be white as you will also have a little line where that rear strap and little buckle have been.

Even worse!

Baseball caps (wrong way around)

What's that all about? People go into shops on holiday to buy a baseball cap and then put it on their head the wrong way around. Why? Wouldn't it be far more sensible just to buy a beret in the first place? Let's try and think through the possible motivations for wearing a baseball cap the wrong way around –

1. You want to look like a drug dealer?
2. You don't wash the back of your neck?
3. You want to look thick?
4. er?

Not much progress there then!

Are there any other possible reasons? If so, I can't think of one. Whether the motivation is 1, 2 or 3, it doesn't really offer a feasible or even half logical reason for this strange pastime so I am obviously missing something.

Bath robes

If you pay a premium and stay in a 'posh' hotel then the chances are that you will be provided with a complimentary bath robe. On the other hand, many people take a bath robe with them on holiday whether they are staying in a posh hotel or not. Be careful unless your room is on the ground floor.

Whether you are staying in a hotel or an apartment block, the chances are that either early morning or early evening, after your shower or bath, you will walk out onto your balcony with a cup of tea or a gin and tonic in your hand. 'Ah, this is lovely. What more could I want? I feel nice and clean and refreshed, the sun is shining and just look at that view'.

Exactly: Just look at that view.

Not your view. The view of the person on the balcony below yours or the person stood in the car park or around the pool below your balcony. 'Oh no; what a bloody sight'. You haven't got any underwear on and you don't realize that anyone below you can see straight up your wotsits.

Sort yourself out; it's not a pleasant sight you know.

Bats and balls

Doesn't it really rattle your tonsils if you're on the beach dozing off when two inconsiderate twonkers come and play bat and ball about six feet away from your sun bed. Aaaaargh – why here next to me? Their family is way over there and yet they have come over here to annoy me. It wouldn't be so bad if someone invented silent bats and balls for the beach, but those wooden bats are infuriating. Apart from all of that, most of them can't play properly anyway and the ball keeps landing on my sun bed. I get wound up and Chris will say to me something along the lines of, 'They're just enjoying themselves. They're on holiday as well you know'. Sack that, next time that ball lands on me it's going into the sea and if the guy says anything then he's following it.

I came on holiday to relax – I think?

Beer strengths

Watch it! A standard lager in the UK is around four percent or just above. Many foreign lagers are considerably higher in alcohol content with five point five or five point six being around the norm. You can watch Brits who are used to drinking five or six pints at home without any problem suddenly going all dollopy on their first day abroad. Five or six pints of this stuff will usually mean that you are well on the way to being completely stupid and a prime candidate for falling over.

Don't drink abroad like you would in the UK or you will almost certainly develop wobbly legs and be able to speak fluent Russian!

Before you leave home

Does your wife do a full spring clean before you go away on holiday? Why is that? Is it in case you are burgled and the robbers might think that you're a set of dirty tatters? Surely it's a good thing if your house is a tip as they are less likely to rob you in the first place. When we lived in the UK and went on holiday, Chris used to walk out of the house backwards with the vacuum cleaner and leave it at the front door.

A trifle excessive don't you think?

Belgians

Have you ever been staying at a hotel and met any Belgians? Aren't they strange? I mean strange in a nice sort of way but they are very withdrawn and - er - well – boring-ish. They never join in anything and if they are in the bar or at an organized evening out, they just sit there with a very occasional tap of the foot to the music. Next time you are on holiday and you see a couple like that, just say to them, 'Excuse me, are you from Belgium?'

If any of you were in your teens during the eighties, you may remember a mad punk rock singer called Plastic Bertrand. He had a couple of hit records and I thought he was fantastic but I think I was the only person in the whole world who ever bought his album. He was more than a little eccentric. Guess what - wow - he was Belgian! Was he the only Belgian who slipped through the 'sensible person' net, because I don't think they make Belgians like him any more?

Plastic Bertrand - Check him out because he's great!

Betty swollocks

Yeah – you know what I mean guys, don't you? Those battery operated mini fans are very useful but you can't use them down the front of your shorts on holiday for two good reasons –

It's dangerous and just the thought of it makes me pull a face like a Japanese fighter pilot.

The noise of the fan and the movement down your shorts would almost certainly get you arrested.

Bidets

Things have changed over the years and its not unusual now for homes in the UK to have a bidet. There are however, still lots and lots of Brits who haven't got a clue what a bidet is used for. We still hear people laughing and saying things like, 'Is it for washing your socks in?' Why, oh why, would they have brought socks with them on holiday anyway? They look stupid.

It's for washing your naughty bits in love!

Binoculars

If you haven't already got a good pair of binoculars then borrow or buy some. You never know what you might see on holiday?

Birdie dance

Nobody watches air hostesses when they're going through the safety procedures and looking like they're doing the birdie dance.

Why? Because people turn a blind eye to the idea of dying. The life jacket bit gets me. What good are a whistle and a tiny little light if you're bobbing up and down in the sea and pooing your pants? Wouldn't two cans of lager and a Mars bar be far more useful, or possibly a spear gun and an outboard motor? I think they should let you take your own life jacket and then you could decide for yourself which accessories suit your own particular dying pattern. You could take this one step further and decide to spend a bit more money on your own personal 'designer' life jacket. You could go with, say, a Manchester United life jacket or a Lacoste life jacket.

Now that's got proper street cred', I mean sea cred!'

Blanket trips

What's it all about – it's silly! In many foreign holiday resorts, particularly in Spain, there are people walking around the streets stopping tourists and asking them if they would like to go on a free blanket trip. The trips are free! They take you on a coach to numerous places of interest on the condition that you visit their blanket showroom as part of the free journey. Now let us assume that you're on your foreign holiday in the middle of August and the temperature is around one hundred degrees (I'm still on Fahrenheit) and they take you to a place that sells blankets - yes, blankets. Who in their right mind wants to buy a blanket when the temperature is melting your flip flops? I can't get my head round it, am I missing something. It just doesn't seem right; not to me anyway.

Oh yes I forgot; the trip is free. That must be why tourists go!

Blubber man

You get on the plane and take your seats. You have usually asked your wife if she would like to sit next to the window and you take the middle seat. 'I hope it's not a full flight and I have a free seat at the side of me'. The plane continues to take on more boarders and then who walks through the door at the front of the plane?

BLUBBER MAN!

Oh no, I hope this big pile of trifle hasn't got the seat next to me. But he has hasn't he. Why is that? It's not fair!

Boats (fishing)

Whenever I go abroad on holiday I look at the little wooden fishing boats near the shore and think how wonderful it would be to do that job. It looks absolutely idyllic, floating around in the sun and pulling a few nets up every now and again. None of this working on a factory ship in the North Sea freezing your wotsits off and stinking of cod – oh no! These guys have got it right, and probably have a fridge in that little hut type thingy on the front full of beer tinnies.

It must be great and I want to do it!

Boats (sardine)

You have probably seen these sardine boats on the beach outside beach bars. They are made of wood and full of sand with sardines cooking in them over a nice fire. These sardine fishermen must be seriously rich people and make a fortune out of sardines. How do they afford it? They go out fishing for sardines in the morning, return to the shore at tea time, fill their boat with sand and then set fire to it. This must warrant a new boat every day and I think boats are quite expensive. A new boat every day – that's serious money!

I wouldn't be surprised if there isn't an EEC grant for boat building and that could possibly explain things?

Boring nerds

If you are a boring nerd, give some thought to other people whilst you are on holiday. They're on holiday as well you know, so don't start talking to strangers in your hotel or in a bar and driving them to distraction. They probably came on holiday in the first place just to get rid of someone like you.

It's very unfair to force your drivel onto other people, especially when they're on holiday, so keep quiet!

Breaking wind in the sea

Have you ever wondered why fishes don't come near the beach? It's not to hide from the fishermen. Fishes are quite clever these days and know that if a worm or a maggot is hanging there in the sea, then it is either well lost or it is on the end of a fisherman's line. No; fishes keep away from the beach because tourists break wind in the water. It's not right! For the sake of all the nice fishes, don't break wind in the sea. You only do it in the sea anyway because you're embarrassed to do it on your sun bed.

Just remember that it's not big and it's not clever to break wind in the sea!

Brothel

The plane smells like one doesn't it. Well, I think it does, as I have never actually been to a brothel – honest! What I should say is that the plane smells like I would imagine a brothel smells because it appears that every single person on the plane has been spraying perfume and after shave all over themselves. Most people do it. They wander into the duty free perfume section and then proceed to squirt themselves with anything they can get their hands on.

It's free, so I'll just have a bit of the lot!

Buckets and spades

Why is it that you can buy plastic buckets and spades in every colour imaginable for children but you can't buy adult buckets and spades? It's not fair! It only appears to be acceptable for children to have buckets and spades on the beach but we men think they're great. If you see a family on the beach with a bucket and spade it is usually the father or grandfather who is doing most of the digging and sand castle building. If there are no children present then these adult men don't use buckets and spades because other people would laugh at them. What's the difference? Why should you have to have a child present in order to enjoy building sand castles? Think about it. It's a fact that if you, as an adult, started digging in the sand on your own with a bucket and spade, then all the other tourists on the beach would laugh and take the mickey out of you – 'Pheeeww, hee hee, look at that big kid over there.' Why can't you buy adult designer buckets and spades in order to make the pastime more acceptable? They could be made in manly colours like black or dark green or a camouflage design.

People wouldn't laugh at me, I mean you, if you could buy blokey ones would they?

Buffet meals in the hotel

Have you seen the fat greedy snorting piglets? They're always there, pushing and shoving in the queue with their tray shaking because they can't wait to get to the grub. They're not necessarily all that hungry, but they want the lot. They pile their food so high on the plate that it looks like a road accident. What's wrong with them? You would think that they had been starved for two days but they did exactly the same at lunchtime and they will do exactly the same for breakfast tomorrow. They don't eat it all – they can't!

Fat belly gut buckets!

Bull fighters (Matadors)

Big headed, bullying (excuse the pun), arrogant, cowardly girlies. They stand there with a big sword wearing incredibly stupid clothes and lady looking socks. They have a large red sheet which they wave around until the bull runs towards it and then stick the sword in the bull. How brave is that then - not very! Do these guys just wake up one morning and think to themselves 'I think I will start wearing stupid clothes in order to look like a weirdo and then act like a weirdo by killing loads of completely innocent bulls? If I do, then I can wear a daft hat as well.' Personally, I would like to see these sadistic girlies get a right good thrutch up the bottom!

I don't like bull fighters you know!

Bulls

They're the big hairy bad assed animals who can't fence; they can't even hold a sword! I am waiting for that freak of nature when the Isaac Newton equivalent of a bull is born in Spain. He will see a few of his mates get wasted by that pink and purple matador twonker, do a few equations on the back of a fag packet, generate a survival plan, nick a gun, and then when the weirdo in pink comes towards him with the sword, Isaac will shoot him between the eyes. Now that's proper star quality! The whole bull ring audience would be shouting, cheering, and throwing their hats into the air. Now if Isaac is really clever then he will have nicked an Uzi machine gun instead of a pistol and will then begin to total the whole crowd as they really came here to see HIM die. Gotcha! That would be proper entertainment wouldn't it. Why haven't the Spanish ever thought of that? I guess they're not very good at lateral thinking.

It's easy: get the bull to kill the matador, because he's a bit of a wassock anyway!

Bum bags

By definition (I think), a bum bag is meant to be near your bum. Lots of people have bum bags for their holidays in order to keep their money and personal belongings safe. They would be safe wouldn't they; who the hell wants to go near a strange persons bum? Take a look next time you go abroad for your holidays. Many very fat men walk around in just a pair of shorts with sandals (sometimes with patterned socks) and their bum bag is under their incredibly fat belly. You can only see a small part of it as the rest is hidden underneath his huge cantilevered gut. I guess he must think it is much safer under his gut near his willy than it would be near his bum. If so, that suggests that a potential thief would rather go near his bum than his willy which doesn't say an awful lot about his willy does it? How would he know anything about his willy anyway, because he probably hasn't seen it for twenty years unless he stands on his head.

I must look in the shops next time I'm in the UK and see if you now have the choice of buying either a bum bag or a willy bag!

Burny burny – ouch – bloody hell!

You're lying on your sun bed on the beach and decide to go for a swim or for a walk to the beach bar. Up you get and walk about ten steps when all of a sudden you realize that the sand is about as hot as hell. 'Ooh, ooh, aaargh, bloody hell!' You just grind to a halt and start jogging on the spot don't you? The problem is that you are half way between where you came from and where you want to be. Whichever way you go, you are going to burn your feet even more. 'Should I leg it back to the sun bed or should I leg it to my destination? Whichever way I choose, I can't win!' It hurts, it hurts a lot and it isn't funny. Unless you see it happening to someone else! In that case it's side slapping funny and you turn around to tell everyone within earshot 'Look at him/her over there burning their feet on the sand – ha ha ha – what a div!'

Surely that's cruel isn't it?

Butter portions

I can understand why they do it, honestly I can. In most foreign holiday destinations the temperature is usually high, so they keep butter portions in the fridge and then bring them out to your table in the hotel dining room in a bowl full of ice cubes – fine! You fish around in the freezing cold water for one of the butter portions and then dribble half a pint of this water onto the table cloth by the time you have wrestled it onto your side plate. You then peel back the little diaphragm lid (if you're lucky) and endeavour to scrape a little bit of the butter onto your knife. Absolutely no chance; not a chance in hell because this butter is about as hard as granite. You can't scrape any of this frozen butter onto your knife so you then get mad and try to dig it out. What's the result? There are a few possibilities actually:

1. The butter flies out of the little plastic container at tremendous velocity and lands on the next table.
2. The knife skims off the butter and sticks into your other hand.
3. The butter shifts sideways, falls into your lap, and your knife goes through the bottom of the little plastic container.
4. You didn't want any butter anyway – sack that!

What can you do in order to get round this incredibly frustrating situation? You could put the knife down your shorts for five minutes or you could put the butter portion down your shorts for five minutes. You could even put them both down your shorts for five minutes.

Either way, it's not very appetising is it?

C

Camcorders

Don't you think the world changed for the worse when they miniaturized camcorders? At present you can buy camcorders which are no bigger than a standard camera used to be, but not long ago they were at least the size of a building brick. I never owned one myself, but have many fond memories of the brick type camcorder hoisted onto the shoulder of some over enthusiastic father. There was nothing better on your annual holiday abroad than to see this guy with his camcorder walking backwards. He would have the camcorder on his shoulder with one eye closed and the other eye stuck into that little rubber hole type thingy. I used to be laughing before it even happened because I knew that at some point during the proceedings the inevitable was going to happen. It was always the most fun if he happened to be near the swimming pool. The camcorder is on his shoulder, one eye goes into the rubber hole and the other eye shuts 'Come on Jimmy, kick the ball, smile son'. He's carried away now and yes, he's walking backwards, go on, a bit further – SPLASH – 'Ha ha, phweeeeeew, hee hee, phweeeeeew'. He's in the pool; you could have taken bets on it. If it wasn't the pool then he would have at least fallen over a sun bed.

Camcorders – they're not funny anymore!

Car hire

As with the holiday rep excursions, car hire is usually more expensive through the holiday rep. They don't do it for nothing,

34

so it has to be cheaper outside by at least the commission that the holiday company is getting. Of course you must be careful and watch out for Paco 'I've got lots of nice cars – honest' Jiminez. He's a robber and actually only has a 1976 Seat Ibiza with wonkey everything. Walk around for a couple of days and have a look. Make sure that the insurance is fully comprehensive and have a look at the standard of cars parked outside. The chances are that you will get a car from the same company that the travel company uses - but cheaper!

Car horns

Ignore them! Foreigners absolutely love their car horns and they are like kids with a new toy. If you are walking down the road or crossing the road and oblivious to the fact that there is a car heading in your direction, you will get silently run over. The driver who kills you will not even think of beeping his horn to warn you of the danger. Oh no, horns are not used for that abroad. They are fun accessories and just there for a laugh really. They are used for beeping non-stop at all their mates, beeping at shop fronts so the lottery ticket man brings one out to his car, beeping at a tourist in a bikini, or just beeping for the sheer hell of it.

As a warning of danger, never. Just ignore them!

Cardboard

With perfume on it!

You see them at every airport in the world; people wandering around with little pieces of cardboard. They have been loitering in the perfume section of the duty free shop and an assistant has collared them. 'Try this one madam; it's new and on special offer'. They spray a little piece of cardboard with the stuff and then wander around with it for three hours, wafting the damn thing in front of them. They don't realize that they still have it. Throw it away, the smell has gone, and you didn't buy any anyway.

You thought it was naff – remember?

Carousels

Why is it that my suitcase always seems to be the last one around the airport carousel? I checked in before that guy there, and I was sat nearer to the exit door on the plane. I can also walk faster than him and I got to the carousel first, but he already has his suitcases and mine aren't here yet. It's unfair! On the odd occasion that my cases aren't last, I can't get to them anyway because of the carousel huggers. These people are complete lunatics, what's wrong with them? He stands there with his legs apart and his hands on his hips in order to take up as much room as possible. If your case comes round before his then he's not going to let you take it off the belt – he wants his first.

Dig him in the ribs, stand on his toe, shout 'FIRE' – moron!

Cars (new)

There aren't any new cars abroad. Well, they are new for about three minutes after driving away from the dealership and then the new car suddenly becomes an old car because it gets bashed. Therefore it looks old. You never see a new car abroad because all the new cars look like old cars. It's not worth taking it in for a re-spray because three minutes after leaving the paint shop it will be bashed again.

Why bother going to the fair when you can play dodgems all day long for nothing abroad.

Cats

It never ceases to amaze me how many UK tourists adopt a foreign cat whilst on holiday. There is absolutely nothing wrong with liking cats but to see some scraggy moggy, start feeding it and falling in love with it is totally beyond me. Believe it or not, some people get so attached to a stray cat on their foreign holiday that they take the poor thing home with them and put it in quarantine for months. This wild animal was perfectly happy before you came along so just leave it alone. Think about it from the cats point of view. It has been completely foot loose and fancy free in a beautiful climate since the day it was born; not a bad life? What are you going to do? Take it back to the UK, buy it a stupid collar, some fluffy toys, and have its wotsits cut off if it's a boy cat or its other bits cut out if it's a girl. You will then let it wander around in the rain and snow and probably get run over.

If you were the cat, which option would you go for?

Ceramic plant pots and wall pots

Brits buy zillions of these things. They are painted in bright coloured patterns and look very – er - foreign – ish! You can watch Brits in foreign markets and souvenir shops buying all the stock. The locals can't make enough of them. People buy these things in a foreign environment when the sun is shining and they look great – ish. The problem is that when you get them home and put or hang them in your lounge or conservatory, they look tacky!

Never mind, give it to your aunty for Christmas.

Chains and padlocks

Who the hell do these hotel swimming pool attendants think they are? You're on holiday and you want to sit round the pool at nine o'clock in the morning. What's wrong with that? Oh no, the swimming pool attendant is the only person who has a key to unlock the sun beds and he or she hasn't arrived yet. Even when they do arrive they start mopping the tiles, wiping the tables or anything they can think of just to infuriate us. Are they jealous because they're not on holiday and we are? Why lock the sun beds up anyway because you're hardly likely to put one in your suitcase and take it home with you - are you?

Foreign swimming pool attendants; I can't stand them.

Chair legs (see also stiletto heels)

Scrape, scrape, scrape – it drives you mad! Why do people scrape chairs across the floor in the room above you (me)? Why doesn't someone invent some kind of rubber stopper thingies to go on the bottom of chair legs, it can't be too difficult, can it? Next time the people in the room above yours start scraping chair legs across the floor, take them up a few packs of condoms, one condom for each chair leg. Don't waste your money buying flavoured ones though because they probably won't be necessary.

You never know though, there are some very strange people around these days!

Changing your trunks (or bikini bottoms)

Whilst on the beach or around the swimming pool it is quite common to see someone trying to change their swimming trunks or bikini bottoms with a towel wrapped around them in order to cover up their modesty. Wow! It's difficult, dangerous and incredibly embarrassing, but very funny indeed as long as it isn't you who is trying to do it.

Round the waist goes the towel, and it's then a quick skeg around to see if anyone is watching. One hand is holding the towel around the waist in case the knot comes loose and then the first leg lifts up. Now it's into hopping mode and the free hand tries to go up the towel and pull the bottoms down but there's a lurch to one side and then three more hops. The towel is starting to drop a little and open at the side, so it's back up with the bottoms and four more hops. This can go on for absolutely ages and the chances are that anyone who is remotely interested will see your naughty bits anyway.

To hell with that! Just drop the towel and if everyone can see your bits, so what?

Chasing flies

With a rolled up newspaper? Forget it!

Most of us do it at some point during our foreign holiday. Flies must surely be the most annoying things in the whole world because they won't take the hint and leave you alone. You can try

38

to kill it twenty seven times in two minutes but it still keeps coming back for more. You will waft it away once, twice, three times, whatever, and then that's it; you're on a mission. Most men head straight for the newspaper and roll it up in order to make a pathetic truncheon type thingy, then dance and chase around the bedroom like a mad dog. I have done it myself on hundreds of occasions and then someone told me that the only way you can hit a fly is from directly overhead. Did you know that? It is a completely futile exercise trying to side swipe a fly. When a fly detects something coming towards it, it quickly takes off *vertically*.

Try it; it works!

Checking your watch

How many times have you seen a man doing that on holiday? Checking his watch late morning whilst sat in a café to see if it's midday yet. Why midday? It's a strange thing; but most men don't believe they should have a pint until midday. You look at your watch and it's ten to twelve; that's the worst possible time it could be! If you have a pint now, you will feel guilty for some unknown reason. Then there is the question of your wife. Midday is a psychological barrier to her as well insofar as she will have a proper monk on if you order a pint at ten minutes to twelve. Best not eh? Ten minutes isn't a long time to wait is it?

Well yes actually. If you want a pint, then ten minutes is a hell of a long time to wait!

Chocolate icebergs

They can't help it! Small children don't always have complete control over their bowels, but oh boy; can they clear a swimming pool. There everyone is, swimming happily in the pool and having a great time when someone suddenly shouts out 'AAARRRGH CHOCOLATE ICEBERG'.

You would think there was a great white shark in the pool!

Cholera

That's 'A man named cholera'. Once you've got him, you can't get rid of him!

Why does he always latch on to me? I haven't said a thing to him but he's taken a verbal fancy to me and he's the most boring person in the whole world. I got his life story on the first day and now I find myself hiding behind pillars in the hotel lobby. I didn't bring a wig and false moustache with me, so I guess that's it for the next two weeks. I try being rude to him but that doesn't work either. He keeps coming back for more.

Cholera – He's like the chimes of a town hall clock; everyone hears him but nobody takes any notice. Watch out for him. He ruins your day, every day.

Clouds

What's so special about clouds when you're on holiday abroad? You can see tourists all day every day on the beach; cloud spotting. They see clouds permanently in the UK and then go abroad cloud spotting as if it's some kind of pastime or therapeutic hobby.

'Ooh look, there's a cloud over there'. Yeah, so what? Give the monkey a peanut for spotting a cloud. Am I missing something or is that plain stupid or what?

Coach (at the foreign airport)

Why do you want to sit on the front seat of the bus? Because you then hope that you will be the first person off the bus. It's a complete waste of time. Similar to the carousel syndrome, it is completely useless being the first person off the bus unless your suitcases are the first ones out of the bus's hold. They never are though; you may as well sit at the back! The front rows of seats on the bus are actually the worst ones to sit on because you are right in the face of the holiday rep. She will get on that microphone telling you the same stuff they told you the last time you went on holiday and being at the front, it nearly deafens you. They are smiling and welcoming you whilst at the same time thinking to themselves, 'Just get to your hotel slap heads, so that I can go out with my mates and get wasted.'

They don't really mean what they say you know!

Cocktails

There are thousands of cocktail bars in the major foreign holiday resorts and thousands more ordinary bars that sell cocktails. They're dangerous you know! We have all done it at one time or another. You have a cocktail. Try another. Giggle. Try another. Then attempt to go to the toilet and fall flat on your face. Never under estimate the strength of those silly looking drinks with a paper parrot sticking out of the top.

I wonder if the name of your cocktail tells you something about yourself. Maybe it tells you something about who or what you would like to be, or the mood that you're in. Most people don't even look at what's in a cocktail; they just go for the name.

Jelly baby	You big kid!
Depth charge	I fancy a curry tonight.
Orgasm	You may be subconsciously thinking to yourself 'Oh yes, I remember one of those - vaguely!'
Bloody Mary	That's boring, unless you fancy punching some poor woman called Mary.
Grand slam	You fancy punching someone even if their name isn't Mary.
Monkey gland	You're sick and require therapy.

Between the sheets	Who with?
Pina Colada	Del Boy, second hand car selling medallion man.
Manhattan	I wish I was in New York.
You're Ugly and your Mum dresses you funny	I just made that one up!

It can sometimes be a major task actually getting the cocktail that you really want to drink. Some of the names are so filthy that you daren't ask for one if you're sober. **IF** you are a **NICE** lady, you are unlikely to walk into a bar and say to the foreign waiter 'Two orgasms please', are you?

You are. Fair enough then!

Cocktail jugglers

They're very clever aren't they? Have you ever seen them doing all that stuff? I sit there completely mesmerized by all that throwing around and juggling type stuff. I daren't do it though because I would spill it and that would be a waste wouldn't it?

Cockroaches (foreign)

Have you seen them? Ooooh! Foreign cockroaches, they scare the hell out of me. Some of them are as big as a Scalextric car. They don't bite people or do them any harm whatsoever, but the fact remains that nearly everyone is seriously poo your pants scared of them. If you see one in your hotel room at night then there is no way that you are going to bed with that big chieftain tank mincing about. What do you do? You try to find some kind of receptacle to push it into and then throw it out of the window. Even if you pretend that you aren't frightened of them, you should watch yourself approaching the cockroach and trying to scoop it up. Just at the last second it legs it and you jump as high as the ceiling and you are now running around like a big Jessy.

Admit it; you are frightened of them really aren't you?

Coffee

'All I want is a coffee, why is it so difficult?'

Have you ever been into a café abroad and seen how many different permutations there are for a coffee? You only want a coffee, but it can take you ten minutes to work your way through the different variations. Depending on where you are there's a sombre, a café con leche, a cortado, an espresso, a café au lait, a cappuccino, an Americana, a solo, bla bla bla.

Sack that, I'll just have a pint, it's far easier!

Coffee and a brandy

Oooh – this is dangerous! I have done it myself lots of times and each time promised myself that I wouldn't do it again; but I did! You get up one morning and think to yourself, 'I fancy a coffee and a brandy.' You order the coffee and brandy and really enjoy them so you then order another coffee and a brandy. It's gone straight into your system and you feel a bit light headed at 9.30 in the morning. 'You go to the beach love and I'll just sit here for another five minutes.' If you manage to get away with that one, then it's another coffee and brandy isn't it? Then another and you're quite blathered by now. It's only mid morning! Oh well, another coffee and another brandy eh? Then what happens? You knock off the coffees. Its brandy only now and by lunch time you're completely and utterly off your trolley, talking and laughing to yourself.

You had better go home to bed now because you're in big trouble!

Colds – don't catch one!

Now here's a thing. I live in Spain and it's probably unfair to say this, but in the winter months when the weather is nice but certainly not what you might call hot, there are Brits walking around in a pair of shorts and no shirt. There are also ladies walking around in a pair of shorts and a bikini top. It's warm(ish), but it obviously appears to be a hell of a lot warmer to them than it does to me. I suppose if you're coming from a minus whatever climate to somewhere with sunny(ish) weather, then it feels warm to you.

Look around. You will see the locals falling about laughing at you because to them, you look like a prat. What the hell; so what!

Cold sores

Do you get them?

You can go through most of your life and then one day there's a bubbling sensation under your lip. It starts off with a little tingle and then rumbles into what seems like a volcano. Then – BANG – it explodes, usually when you're in a restaurant having your dinner and you think an alien has just come up your throat. 'Bloody hell – aaaaargh!' Who gave you the cold sore in the first place? Apparently they lie dormant under your lip for ages and then just erupt every now and again, usually on your holidays. You often see holiday makers who look as though they've just gone five rounds with Mike Tyson.

It's not funny!

Compulsive disorders

How do these people go on when they go abroad on their holidays? It's no laughing matter. It is a genuine illness and these people can't help continually checking to make sure that the door is shut or they are continually checking that their flies are zipped up properly. It can take on all forms of compulsive checking, double checking and double double checking. Apparently most of these checks take place in their own home, so how do they carry on when they're on holiday in a hotel or apartment? There are lots and lots of doors in hotels and apartment blocks and it would be a full time job going around checking them all and then checking them all again. Besides that, every door in the place except one belongs to someone else. You would get locked up surely?

As for continually checking to see if your flies are fastened on holiday. Well, that's a definite lock up isn't it?

Copies

You can buy copies of virtually anything you want in many foreign holiday resorts. You will read in this book about rip off sun glasses, shirts, CD's etc. The fact is that you can buy virtually any product with virtually any designer logo on it that you care to name. Don't believe everything you see abroad when it comes to the designer logo. Just because that mans shirt has a Lacoste logo on it, it doesn't necessarily mean that it really is a Lacoste product. Just because that mans watch says TAG on it, it doesn't necessarily mean that it really is a TAG product. Don't always believe what you read or see abroad.

It says OXO on the side of buses, but I've never seen a bus selling OXO. Have you?

Corridor tig

Why do children do it? More to the point; why do their parents allow them to do it?

Children go on holiday to a beautiful hot climate; their accommodation almost certainly has at least one swimming pool, a play area, children's club, table tennis tables and just about everything a kid could possibly want. What do they do? I'll tell you what they do; they play bloody tig in the corridor outside my room! I can be on the first floor or the tenth floor, but I always seem to get the little ankle snappers continually running up and down my corridor. Why me; because I'm a very nice man – I think?

You have to give children a little licence, but when it's outside my room whilst I'm trying to have a little kip then all sorts goes through my mind -

1. Leave them alone. They're only having a little bit of fun.
2. Let them have their half an hours run about. They will get bored soon and go away.
3. Their parents won't let them carry on like this for long. I'm sure they will come and get them in a minute?
4. Open the door and tell them to sod off.
5. Go into town, buy some fishing line and make a trip wire across the corridor (outside someone else's room).
6. Go out for a few beers?

That's it then. Its number 6!

Counting down the weeks

I used to do it and I think most people do because once you have actually booked your holiday; you want to go as soon as humanly possible. It's thirteen weeks next Monday until you go. When it gets to next Tuesday you're telling everyone that it's now only twelve weeks to your holiday. It isn't twelve weeks at all, its twelve weeks and six days but twelve weeks sounds nearer – TO YOU!

You're wishing your life away you know!

Crapple rumble

In the UK you see cafes with little glass or Perspex thingies on the counter with all kinds of yummy looking puddings and cakes in them. That's fair enough in the UK climate, but in hot foreign holiday resorts where the sun is melting the tarmac, these puddings can't be fresh can they? To make matters worse, instead of proper cream you get a dollop of that sympathetic cream and it's atrocious.

Apple crumble? Crapple rumble more like 'Buoooooogh!'

Crisps

I can't stand it. When someone buys a packet of potato crisps and they sit next to me in a bar. Why can't they suck them? Rattling the bag and crunching the crisps; it ruins my holiday and I want to take the crisps off them and shove them where the sun don't shine.

Or is it just me?

If I buy a packet of crisps in a bar I try to eat them as quietly as I can without infuriating fellow customers. Even then, I usually get annoyed but for a completely different reason. I like to think that I'm not a selfish person and, as such, if I buy a packet of crisps I always offer one to the people who I am with. What happens? I'll tell you what happens. They won't buy a packet of crisps themselves, but when I offer them my packet they shove their hand in the packet and take a fist full. It's then on to the next person who may be more polite and just takes one or refuses with a 'Thank you' and then the next person who also takes a fist full.

The greedy gannets. I bought the things and now I've only got a few scrag ends left in the bottom of the packet 'Aaaaaaaargh!' I hate crisps!

Crowns and bridges

If you have a dental crown or a bridge in your mouth then you can go for five years and never have any problems whatsoever. You can't even remember that you have a few crowns and bridges. Why is it then that if your crown or your bridge drops out it's usually whilst you are on holiday. You can be eating a sandwich or chewing gum with only a couple of days of your holiday gone when its 'What the hell; what's this in my sandwich?' You spit the offending item out into your hand and it's one of your crowns. You then panic because you now know that for the rest of your holiday you will look like a complete gimpy with a big gap between your teeth. When you try to talk there's air blowing through the gap and depending on the position of the gap, you may start slavering.

47

Do you spend the next ten days or so telling people that your crown dropped out or do you risk the foreign dentist? Not a great choice!

Cuttings

Why do some people go on holiday and take cuttings of foreign flowers. They can be lying around the pool, driving in the foreign countryside, or simply lying on the beach. 'That's a nice flower isn't it?' They take a cutting, soak it in water and then wrap it in newspaper to take home to the UK.

It dies. Now there's a shock!

D

Deaf beggars

These people wander around most foreign holiday resorts. They go into restaurants and bars placing a piece of paper on each table explaining the fact that they are deaf and asking for a donation. Shortly after we moved to Spain we were in a bar when one of these people came in. I was about to give a small donation when Chris' son, Jonathan, told me that most (not all) were complete fakes. 'Oh that's a bit cynical', I said. 'Okay, watch this' said Jonathan. He got out of his chair and walked around the beggar to sneak up behind him. **<u>'BOO'</u>** he shouted at the top of his voice. This poor guy nearly followed through and jumped about two feet into the air.

Point proven I guess!

Didn't hurt – honest!

You've done it and you must have seen lots of other people doing it as well?

You're in the sea splashing around and having a great time. You then decide that enough is enough and that you will go back and have a little lay down on your sun bed for a while. The problem is that when you are walking out of the sea, you tread on a sharp stone or something which doesn't feel quite right and then fall over. You fall over onto stones or shingle and it hurts like hell; in fact it really really hurts. What do you do? You stagger around and look at everyone else on their sun beds and you laugh! 'Ha ha' – to nobody in particular because you feel a right plonker! On the other hand, they have seen you fall over and they want to laugh but daren't for some reason. As far as everyone (including you) is concerned; it never happened. You then try to stand tall and saunter back to your sun bed with a smile on your face, 'Dee, dee dee, dee dee'. Once you get there, you bury your head into your towel and its 'Aaaargh – ******* – that really ******* hurt, but I didn't show it, did I?'

Yes you did!

Dire Straits

Do you get all giggly on the run up to your foreign holiday? Most people do. You have already told half the population of Britain that you're going away on holiday and you're really getting into the mood now. You're almost on the beach already, you can smell the sea.

Go on, put Dire Straits 'Twisting by the pool' on your music system – high volume! The noise will really naff your neighbours off and it will also make them incredibly jealous. If you have a neighbour who you don't speak to, then it will let them know that you're going on holiday and really really really naff them off. Timing is crucial with the neighbours you don't speak to depending on how bitter and twisted they are. If you leave high volume 'Twisting by the pool' until a couple of days before your departure date then they're not likely to retaliate until you've already gone away.

Good eh?

'Do you live here?'

Come on, think about it. It's not logical, so don't do it!

If you go into a British bar or restaurant on your holiday abroad and get talking to the owner or to one of the staff, don't ask them the question which they hate most of all, 'Do you live here?' I know you're only trying to be friendly and it's probably the first thing that comes into your head – but!

Do you really think they commute from a UK airport every day?

Dog poo

I know it's not a pleasant subject but it has to be mentioned because it's important. Watch out for it abroad. It is a cast iron fact that if you see a British ex pat, or any other northern European ex pat' for that matter, out walking their dog abroad, they will inevitably have a little bag with them in order to pick up anything their dog decides to deposit on the pavement. Not the locals, oh no. There's no excuse for it but the thought doesn't even enter their heads. If there were dog poo wardens abroad going around continually cleaning the stuff up then you could half understand it, but there aren't. Result – dog poo on the pavements.

Shed loads of it. Watch out!

Dogs (Mediterranean)

For some reason which I can never fathom out, many Mediterranean's who own a dog have these extremely ugly hairy little things. They have buck teeth that stick out in all directions, yap all the time, have dirty matted hair and nothing going for them whatsoever. They look a bit like one of those peekawotsit hairdresser prostitute type dogs but with bad attitude. They are horrible and I guess there must be some sound reason why the Mediterranean's like them, but Christ knows what that reason is.

If the name hadn't already been taken by another incredibly ugly breed of dog, then they would probably have been called Shiatsu's.

Dogs (foreign airports)

Have you ever noticed when you come through to the arrivals

51

hall in a foreign airport, there are always ex pats waiting for their friends or relatives who have one or more dogs with them? Why? Do they stand there saying to the dog 'Only a few minutes now, watch the door, your uncle Bert will come through it in a minute?'

Are they right in their heads or what?

Dollop (Mr. and Mrs.)

If you go on a package holiday then inevitably there will be a Mr. and Mrs. Dollop staying in your hotel. Usually they are actually very nice people but they're just – er - dollops. They keep themselves to themselves to the extent that you sometimes think they're dead. They may shake their head every now and again, but they don't appear to have the ability to speak. They look lethargic, do everything at a snails pace and never say a word to anyone, including each other. I suppose they must be quite happy in their own little way, but it's a shame they don't attempt to break out of this dollop mode.

Underneath that dollop exterior, they could find that they are actually really side slapping funny people.

Dolphin trips

I think dolphins are great, but I have never seen one apart from on the TV. Many foreign holiday resorts run dolphin trips but I never see any dolphins. I can talk to just about every other tourist in the resort and they have all seen the dolphins. However, every time I go out the dolphins appear to have a meeting amongst themselves and say something along the lines of 'Quick, Stuart Wright's here – leg it!' Why do they always hide when I go out to see them because I like them?

The last time Chris and I went on a dolphin trip I got told off. As soon as we walked up the gang plank of the boat I asked where the bar was, 'Is that all you ever think about, beer'. Er, no not really, it's just that I believe the bar tender is also the safety officer so I thought I could get to know him just in case – honest!'

Safety first. What's wrong with that?

Domestic (in the room next door)

Has it ever happened to you? There you are enjoying your holiday when all of a sudden world war three breaks out at three o'clock in the morning in the room next door. It starts with a bang, then a woman shouting, then a crash, then a guy shouting and bawling, then another bang, then the woman starts shouting and crying both at the same time. There you are laid in bed wondering what the hell is going on. More shouting, more banging, more crying and it's doing your head in now, but you don't know what to do. Is the guy beating the woman up? It sounds like it. Should I go round, bang on the door and ask the lady if she's okay? If I do that; what are the possibilities –

1. How big is the bloke and will he take a swing at me?
2. How big is the woman and will she take a swing at me?
3. They could just tell me to **** off and mind my own business.
4. The woman could be really grateful that someone has saved her from a beating.
5. It could be the woman who is beating the guy up – it happens!

I think I'll just phone reception. That way the nice reception guy gets a slap instead of me.

'I'm on holiday you know!'

Donkeys

To many foreigners, donkeys are the lowest form of life. For instance: the word 'donkey' in Spanish is 'burro' and to call someone a burro is a bigger insult than calling them a fat lump of poo. Why is that? Donkeys are nice. We Brits like them a lot, but foreigners don't. We give them sweets or a sugar lump whilst the locals kick hell out of them and tie them in the middle of a field with a piece of old rope and no shade whatsoever. Okay, they might sometimes put a shabby straw hat on the poor donkeys head as a special treat, but I don't think its to take their guilt away. I hate people who ill treat donkeys nearly as much as I hate bull fighters. Possibly I'm too soft and live in the wrong country. Should I move to a country where they are kinder to animals like Iran, Kosovo or Afghanistan?

They're absolutely horrible to people, but I think they like donkeys.

Door pocket gear changes

They drive on the other side of the road abroad you know. I have done it myself and it cracks me up. Most people, when they first collect a hire car on their foreign holiday, set off and then go into the door pocket in order to change gear.

All you will find in there are some old sweets!

Do you speak English?

Be very careful with a foreigner who says he only speaks a little English. Tourists go into bars and shops asking the local, 'Do you speak English?' Inevitably the reply you get will be 'A little'. They don't mean it. When they say 'A little', what they usually mean is 'A lot'. Don't be the smarty pants who turns around to his mate and says something like 'Idiot; he won't know what I'm talking about'. He will you know!

Remember, when it comes to a foreigner saying he only speaks a little English, he really means a lot. Don't insult him or her. You might get twonked!

Drinking phrases (useful translations)

Personally, I think it is absolutely disgusting for people to get drunk on holiday. We do however live in a democracy, so who am I to pass judgment on these poor people. So as not to leave them out, I list below a few phrases which may come in handy for people who get drunk on holiday. I suggest prior to going away, you go onto the Internet and have these phrases translated in order for you to take them with you -

'What are you looking at?'

'Help, I'm going to throw up in a minute!'

'Did you just call my pint a puff?'

'You want how much?'

'Stop ogling my missus!'

'Ouch – he just smacked me!'

I wouldn't have any use for these translations myself - but you might?

What you can also do which can be quite funny is this –

Before you leave home, get a felt tip pen, cut up a few cornflake boxes and make some flash cards with the above translated phrases on them. When you're in a foreign bar, use the flash cards instead of actually saying the phrases because you will probably get the pronunciation wrong anyway. If you flash a card or two at a big local when you're wrecked and he comes over to you looking as though he may hit you, then point to a guy on the next table and tell the local that the cards belong to him. That way, the guy on the next table gets smacked instead of you!

Drinks inflation

I don't know how they get away with it?

In the UK the price of a drink is the price of a drink and that's about it isn't it? It may be a fair price or it may be a ridiculously expensive rip off price, but you vote with your feet and if it's a rip off price they'll only get one drink out of you and then you're off. In many foreign holiday resorts, however, there appears to be no legislation about this and you can be sat in a popular British bar at half past six having paid three euros for a pint and then go back to the bar at five past seven for another pint and the price has gone up to four euros. At Nine o'clock it goes up to five euros and then at eleven o'clock it goes up again – and again – and again. How do they justify that then?

What price are the drinks at daft o'clock?

Drip, drip, drip

Why aren't there any beer mats abroad?

You can go into virtually any pub you like in the UK and there will be absorbent beer mats spread all over the tables and along the bar. Abroad however, you hardly ever see a beer mat. Why is that? When you're on your foreign holiday the weather is usually hot and your drink is usually very cold; result – condensation on your glass. There you are in your new smart cotton shirt and tailored shorts. Your wife is wearing her favorite dress. What happens? Drip, drip drip. Your glass is dripping water at a tremendous rate of knots and you usually resort to holding the glass at arms length and then trying to lean forward two feet in order to connect your mouth to the glass without dripping all over your clothes. You look like some kind of retarded circus act and it's not funny.

Well it is actually, if you're watching someone else doing it!

Drive to the airport (in your own car)

Wow – the horns are out - I have done it myself lots of times. You leave home for the drive to the airport and your personality changes beyond imagination. Michael Schumacher has got nothing on you; he's a slow coach. Honk honk -'GET OUT OF THE BLOODY WAY' - 'WHERE'S THAT IDIOT GOING'? - 'I'M COMING THROUGH'. What's happened to you, you're a raving lunatic and you don't normally drive like that. Do you? You have waited all year for this holiday in the sun and now you're trying to kill yourself and half the population of the UK. Your stress level has gone through the roof and why the hell are you rushing so much anyway because you're not late. When you do get to the airport, all you are going to do is queue again, but at least you can get mad in the queue at Check In. It's not a brilliant choice really is it? Would you rather be raving mad sat driving your car, or raving mad stood at the Check In queue?

It's safer at the airport – I think?

Duo toilets

Now this is incredibly confusing – I think so anyway. You can walk into the men's toilet in many foreign bars and there is a sit down toilet on one wall and also a urinal on the wall next to it. What do you do? I only want a wee wee so I won't be using the sit down toilet. Do I lock the door or leave it unlocked? I feel selfish locking the door to a two man toilet but if I don't lock the door, the last thing I want is for some guy to come in, drop his trousers and sit down next to where I'm having a wee wee.

It's not right and it's very confusing!

Dustbin men

They work nights abroad you know!

When you arrive at your hotel or apartment building, look out of your bedroom window immediately. Are there any dustbins within earshot of your room? If there are then you're in deep trouble because dustbin men abroad work during the night! You will be in a deep peaceful sleep at two or three o'clock in the morning when Paco and Manuel or Stavros and Manolis the bin men arrive. They don't give a damn if they wake you up; in fact they want to wake you up.

Why should you sleep when they have to work?

Duty free shops

Don't you find it confusing going into the airport duty free shop these days?

Is it duty free or isn't it duty free? It depends on where you're going to. On the other hand, it also depends where you are coming from. If you're flying out of a UK airport to Spain, Italy, Greece or another Eurozone destination these days, the chances are that you won't be buying any cigarettes or spirits because they're extortionate. Conversely, if you are flying back from that country to the UK, then the chances are that you will have a shed full of both cigarettes and spirits. It's exactly the same journey but the other way around – it's absolutely crazy.

That aside, we all have a little wander around the duty free shop anyway, and often buy something as an impulse purchase even if we don't really want or need it. The favourite impulse purchase is perfume and/or after shave I guess, 'Oooh, that's nice, I think I'll treat myself'. The problem is, and this is a blokey thing, I truly believe that perfume house brand managers and marketing managers must all be women. It is perfectly correct and understandable that ladies fragrances should be called nice flowery romantic type names. There is nothing a lady likes more than for another lady or a man to say to her something along the lines of, 'What's that perfume you're wearing; it smells absolutely gorgeous?' Mission accomplished, well done. However, we men don't want nice ponsy names on our after shave lotions. It would be far more fun and sales generating if you could get men's fragrances with such names as, er, for instance –

Tramps Toilet by Calvin Klunk

Davids Dandruff by Georgio I'mbarmy

Brickies Bum by Yves Smasher

Testosterone by Karl Lagerfellover

Stadium Turf by Hugo Toss

Those kinds of names and manufacturers have far more appeal to men. It would give you tremendous street cred' to walk into your local pub and your mates say –

'Phwooooagh, Stuart, what's that you've got on?'

'Oh, it's my new after shave called Tramps Toilet by Calvin Klunk'.

'Blimey, it's terrible: I must get some'.

Yeah, blokey after shaves. Let's have some.

E

Ear plugs (During August)

If you go abroad during the month of August then ear plugs are absolute 'must' accessories. Foreign industry just about closes during the month of August and many, if not most foreigners, head for the local coast for their annual month's holiday. They shout, they shout a lot. You can be on the beach, in a restaurant, on a pleasure boat, or anywhere you care to name on a foreign coast and you will experience a complete and utter ear bashing. Foreigners are completely incapable of having a nice quiet conversation, they just shout. You will probably think that they're arguing but it's just normal behavior to them.

Take some ear plugs because they do your head in!

Ear plugs on the plane

Some people suffer from severe headaches during take off and landing on aircraft and we have to sympathize with these poor unfortunate people. In order to overcome the problem, some altitude sufferers use these spongy ear plug thingies which are usually bright yellow. Have you seen them? You can be sat there on the plane minding your own business and having a quick gander at the other travellers when all of a sudden your eyes lock onto the person sat opposite to you. What's wrong with their head? Is their brain melting? These bright yellow spongy bungy thingies have started to work their way out of this persons ears and they look as though they have some radio active gunk coming out of their head.

'Oh, it's just some of those spongy bungy thingies; thank God for that!'

Elastics gone!

Is it the salt water, the sun, or is it foreign washing powder? Most men these days wear swimming shorts but if you are a 'Speedo trunks man' or a lady, then the chances are that the elastic in your trunks, swim suit or bikini bottoms will go all baggy during your annual holiday. It can be embarrassing when you come out of the sea or swimming pool and then suddenly realize that you have developed low slung swim suit bottoms. The gusset is about two kilos heavier because you have three pints of sea water in it. You can sometimes watch people coming out of the sea or the swimming pool walking like a hermit crab and looking all self conscious – 'Oops – elastics gone!'

It's not only the embarrassment either, because you know damn well that you will now get sand up your bottom and your wobbly bits!

Emergency every day phrases

Depending on who you are and what you do on holiday, there are every day phrases which you may find useful (see also drinking phrases). Obviously I cannot cover the whole spectrum of potential circumstances but here are a few for emergency use that you should translate prior to departure –

'Where can I buy some HRT tablets for my wife? Please – hurry up!'

'I've just chopped my finger off on the sun bed, get a doctor quickly!'

'I'll have chips with mine.'

'**** me a jelly fish has just ******* stung me – *******!' (see 'Jelly fish' they make you swear a lot!)

60

'Could we have another toilet roll please?'

'I requested a sea view and all I can see are dustbins.'

'Waiter – there are twenty seven flies in my soup. Oh, and a tab end!'

English pubs

Come on, let's talk this one through. What exactly is an 'English pub?'

You hear people on holiday saying things like 'there's an English pub down the road', or you can actually be walking down a road in your resort and you will see a sign saying 'English pub'. What's one of those please? It is usually a bar just the same as all of the other bars but it has an English flag hanging outside and is owned by an English person. That's it – big deal! What about an Irish pub? Whenever I have been into an Irish pub whether it be in France, Spain, Italy, England or Ireland for that matter, they are just pubs with bare floor boards and Guinness memorabilia hanging all over the place. Oh yes, and the owner is *sometimes* Irish. The same goes for a Scottish pub. That usually has a flag of St. Andrew hanging outside, sells McEwans lager, has three hundred different brands of whisky on the shelf and usually one of those ginger 'See you Jimmy' wigs hanging on the wall. Really original that is! What about a Welsh pub then; what's one of those? I've never seen a Welsh theme pub. I think the Welsh must be the only people in the UK sensible enough to realize that a pub is a pub is a pub – isn't it? I don't think it will take very long for this strange territorial theme for pubs to go one step further. If it does, then it will almost certainly be based on bygone romantic visions of local culture.

There could, for instance, be a Yorkshire pub which might have, let's say, two tons of nutty slack piled outside the door and all the staff wearing miners helmets.

What about a Cumbrian pub, with a highly radio active interior called the Sellafield Arms?

A Birmingham pub with two Austin Allegro's and a Triumph Herald rag top on the roof - 'rusty of course!'

I'm enjoying this - - - -

How about a Lincolnshire theme pub with no bar, no tables, no chairs, no anything – just completely flat?

A Cornish pub where you get a free pasty with every pint and all the staff have a piece of straw hanging out of their mouths?

A Gretna Green theme pub would be good. You could take your girlfriend there and go through a mock marriage whilst having a few beers. You could get dressed up in a top hat and tails with your girlfriend in a full wedding gown with veil and go through a pretend wedding service. It would be very convenient because you are in a pub and after the mock wedding service you could just go to the bar and get completely legless. No need for any pretend wedding cars or anything. On top of all that, to make things even better, when you have an argument afterwards you can just walk away because it wasn't a proper wedding at all. No expensive divorce costs, splitting the house in half, arguing over the bank account – nothing!

Let's have a Kent theme pub. That could have a tractor for the bar, fresh vegetables piled in one corner and illegal immigrants climbing out of a tunnel in the other corner.

Someone could open a Bradford theme pub. I was born in Bradford – best not!

Euros

The Euro has got a lot to answer for when it comes to us not being able to pretend to be millionaires any more. It's just not the same going out for a meal in the likes of Italy or Spain. I have fond memories of going out for an evening meal, probably washed down with a nice bottle of wine and the bill being something like ten zillion Pesetas or Lira. On would go my 'I'm a millionaire head' and I would just recline back and count out the ginormous denomination notes as if they were nothing (actually, they were next to nothing). 'Oh, that's quite reasonable old chap' I would say. At that point in time you could then make a big issue out of leaving a tip which appeared sufficient to buy a brand new family car. 'Oh keep the change dear man' and then swagger out as if you owned the world.

Meanwhile – the waiter would be scowling after you as that huge tip was only actually worth about ten pence – 'Oy, you tight English tosser!'

Excursions from the holiday rep

What a rip off they are, they're like licenced bandits. I reckon that tour operators must make more money out of organized excursions than they do from selling you a holiday in the first place. The reason they bash your ear on the first day of your holiday is because they know that by your second or third day, you will have seen the same trip for half the price at a local travel agents shop.

Say no - you don't have to go on their trips!

Exercises (pre holiday)

Why is it that many people go into a frantic pre holiday exercise burst only two weeks prior to departure? They have known that they are fat all year and what are they going to do about it in two weeks anyway – nothing! They may feel as though they are at least making an effort and getting rid of a bit of guilt, but it's fairly futile really. If you feel a little embarrassed when you look at yourself naked in the mirror then the chances are that you are what in medical terms is called - a fatty.

It takes all year to get rid of all that blubber and two weeks just ain't good enough!

F

Falling over

Wherever you go abroad, be very careful not to trip over anything or fall over in the street. It doesn't matter if there are road works, cracks in the pavement, banana skins, broken bottles or anything else you care to name. If you are looking for an apology from the council or compensation; forget it. It doesn't matter whose fault it was, as far as anyone abroad is concerned if you fall over, it's your fault. 'You should look where you are going'.

That seems fair enough to me!

Fashion police

Why aren't there any?

Have you seen them? It shouldn't be allowed. Some people go on holiday to the sun and dress up like proper wassocks. That kind of bad taste shouldn't be allowed and you should be able to call the fashion police to take them away for a good talking to. If a person goes on holiday by themselves, then I guess there is half an excuse as there is nobody to tell them just how stupid they look. Most however, have a husband, wife or partner and why doesn't that person refuse to walk the streets with them? Even worse, you sometimes see a pair of them and it appears that they are having a competition to see who can look the most stupid!

Bring on the fashion police! That's not unfair - is it?

Fast food

They're having a laugh aren't they? Why is it that you can go into any of the major burger chains in the UK and walk out with your chosen meal within a few minutes of ordering it, and yet abroad you have to wait forever? In the UK they stack and rack the burgers ready for instant service, whereas over there, when you do eventually catch the persons attention they appear to make everything to order. There can be a queue (of sorts) out of the main door but the holding trays are all empty. Every five minutes or so a solitary burger will come dawdling down the chute but it will then sit there for another five minutes until someone notices it. On top of all that, the staff behind the counter are in anything but a hurry. There they are chatting, looking confused, and instant service appears not to be part of their purpose in life.

If you want fast food abroad, then don't go to a fast food restaurant. It would be quicker to cook it yourself!

Favourite British sweets

Take some of yours – yum yum! You can get certain British sweets abroad but not many. If, for instance, you are a Dolly Mixture or a Midget Gem fan then you can forget it. I am not a massive sweet eater but I absolutely love Liquorice Allsorts and although I don't eat them very often, I seem to go into panic mode if I can't have any. I can take a big bag of Liquorice Allsorts on holiday with me and never even touch them but that's not the point, at least I can have some if I want them. Whilst I'm on the subject – why is it that I only ever seem to get one blue Bertie Bassett in each bag I purchase? I love those little blue jelly liquorice tasting Berties, but I only seem to get one in each bag or box.

Are you supposed to only get one in every bag or is there someone on the packing line who nicks all the Berties and eats them? It's not fair!

FIRE!

Where are the external fire escapes abroad? Do you know why you don't see external fire escapes running down the side of foreign apartment blocks? Because there aren't any that's why. It's a complete shambles. Thank God there aren't many serious fires, but if you're on a high floor level and there's a fire you're in big trouble. One of the first things to go off in a fire situation is the electricity and I have never seen any gas operated lifts over there. It's the stair case or jump. This is not a laughing matter, and the foreign authorities need to get their acts together. Do they really think that we Brits bring hang gliders and rope ladders with us on holiday - or is it just that we tourists are dispensable?

Fishermen on the beach

I'm not a fisherman but fishing is apparently Britain's most popular sport and I have to say that it looks quite relaxing. Fair enough. However, have you ever watched fishermen fishing from the shore whilst you're on holiday? More to the point, have you ever seen one of these guys actually catch anything? Most of them seem to stand there for hour after hour and never catch a thing. If they do catch something, it is inevitably a fish that resembles a tiddler. The hook is nearly as big as the fish so they rip half of its face off and then throw it back. When the poor thing grows up it will have a hair lip and a lisp won't it?

It doesn't seem to be a very fruitful way to spend your holiday really!

Flies

They drive me crazy! (see also mosquito's)

I hate flies, but for some reason, presumably the warmer climate, there appear to be millions more flies abroad than there are in the UK. It's incredibly annoying when flies are screaming around you, but it's also incredibly funny to watch other people reacting to the flies. Some people just lose the plot completely and appear to turn into Bavarians within a few seconds. Just put a pair of leather lederhosens on them and there you have him; the fully blown Bavarian arm and leg slapping silly dancer! He (or she) starts with a waft, then a double waft, then a 'phwuuuuu, phhhuuuut' out of the corner of the mouth, and then he's off. Swipe, kick, leg slap, arm slap, head slap: he's now a full blown Black Forest happy slappy dancer but this one wears Hawaiian shorts and flip flops.

Whilst on the subject of flies; have you ever gone to a shop out of sheer frustration on holiday and bought a fly swat? Flies must recognize fly swats because if you acquire one, the flies don't come anywhere near you. It's strange that; flies must be more intelligent than we give them credit for.

Flight calls

Most people do it and it isn't wrong. You leave your car in the long stay car park, get a taxi to the airport, ask a relative to drop you off, catch a bus, whatever. You then queue to dump your bags and secure a boarding card – 'Aah – that's it – aah – I'm on holiday now.' You then go through to the departure lounge, have a wander around and buy a couple of drinks. 'Aah – I'm on holiday now, I'm relaxed.' You have another wander around and possibly another couple of drinks, then – **'Oh my God – er – ooh - look up there on the screen – ooh – er - the gate number's up – quick – er - leave your drinks, the gate number's up!'** People panic, they leg it as if their lives depended on it to the allocated departure gate. The plane isn't going anywhere for absolutely ages; in fact it probably hasn't even arrived yet from wherever it is coming from.

Why do tourists always leg it to the departure gate as soon as their flight appears on the screen. Relax, finish your drink – what's the rush?

Flip flops

I'm okay in a pair of real leather sandals during the baking

67

foreign heat, but rubber flip flops? I can't wear those can you? My feet stick inside the stupid things and they draw my feet like hell. I see other men wearing them and they're walking along the promenade as if they're wearing snow shoes. It looks like a real effort for them just to walk and they appear to be bent forward as if they're walking into a strong head wind. They are almost forcing themselves forward and scraping the stupid floppy rubber things along the ground. If the flip flops are old and lop sided then it's even worse. Their legs are wobbling and they just don't look right. Besides all of that, it's dangerous to wear flip flops on your holiday during July and August because the hot foreign sun melts them.

They're stupid!

Flying

It is a fact of life that some people are afraid of flying. Don't be! Just keep telling yourself over and over again that you can only die once. That should make you feel a lot better.

I think?

Foldy back sun beds

They should actually call these things 'chop your fingers off sun beds' or 'amputation clamps'. It's as though these things have a brain and a terrific sense of humour. If you try to adjust the height of the back of your sun bed then the chances are that it will amputate a finger, a hand or a full arm. It hurts like hell. You can almost hear the sun bed laughing at you. If you're lucky enough to adjust the back without it trapping something or other then it is only lulling you into a false sense of security. It waits one, two or three minutes and then – CRASH – the back drops down. You then fly backwards with your legs in the air, and swear a lot.

It got you again; you knew it would but you didn't quite know when!

Football (Foreign)

Oh dear – watch out pal! Be careful wearing a Real Madrid shirt in Barcelona or a Barcelona shirt in Madrid. Until I came to live in Spain I didn't realize how much hatred there is between the cities of Barcelona and Madrid. Barcelona is the capital of Catalonia which considers itself to be a separate country and even has its own language-ish. Madrid, on the other hand, is the capital of Spain and they don't consider the Catalans to be Spanish either. Confused? Let me put this into perspective. If an English football team is playing Barcelona in the European championships then everyone in Madrid will be cheering for the English club. If, on the other hand, Real Madrid were playing an English team in the same competition, Barcelona would be cheering for the English team. They can't stand each other and consider each other to be foreigners.

Similar situations exist in Italy, Turkey and Greece. It's only a game isn't it? No!

Football (on TV)

Whilst on holiday most men like to watch the odd game of football on the TV. Why not? You will walk along the seafront in your foreign holiday resort and inevitably see a sign outside one of the British bars advertising a game that evening. You show an interest in watching the game and what do you get from your wife or partner? 'Football! I'm sick of football; it's always on the television'. Now come on ladies! Women always come out with the same stock statement, 'Football's always on the TV'. They never mention soaps do they! Think about it. There isn't a day goes by when there aren't at least four soaps on the TV and that's quite literally three hundred and sixty five days of the year. Soaps – all day, every day!

That's different is it?

Foreign food – yuk!

How can you possibly know if you don't try it? It is absolutely amazing, the number of Brits who say 'I don't like foreign food'. If you then ask them if they have tried so and so, they say 'No'. How the hell do you know then? Go on, try them. If you have taken the time to visit a foreign country then at least give their food a try. In all likelihood you will be pleasantly surprised.

Go on, be a devil, try it – buoooooogh!

Foreign people

The merits or otherwise of foreign people is a major topic of conversation amongst British people whilst on their holiday. 'Aren't they ignorant' or 'They're lovely friendly people' depending on the experience someone has had with the locals. It's quite simple really. Wherever you go in the world there are friendly people and there are unfriendly people. There are polite people and there are ignorant people. It's no different in the UK than it is in Greece and it's no different in Peru than it is in Iceland. Generally speaking, if you are nice and polite to people then they are nice and polite to you. Conversely; if you are sharp and ignorant to people then they are sharp and ignorant to you.

Foreign people are no different to everyone else really. Or are they?

Fresh fish and molluscs

Oh, poor things!

I absolutely love fish and seafood in general – but! Have you ever been into one of those sea food restaurants abroad where they have huge tanks full of live fish, crabs and lobsters? I just can't do it. Give me any fish or shell fish cooked on a plate or platter and I will enjoy every single mouthful, but once I see them swimming around and looking at me then that's it, I'm out of there. I just couldn't go up to one of those tanks and choose a fish for them to kill and serve to me on a plate within fifteen or twenty minutes.

As for the restaurant owner, chef and waiters; I just cannot comprehend how they manage to sleep at night. If it was me, then I would finish up giving names to all the fishes and molluscs and falling in love with them. I would probably have a favourite and call him something like Eric or Bob. What do you do then; it wouldn't be very good for business would it? If someone came into the restaurant and wanted to eat poor old Eric then I would probably have to kill them instead! 'How dare you ask me to kill Eric; what's he ever done wrong to you?'

Next time you go into one of these foreign seafood restaurants, just spare a thought for Eric because he's a very nice lobster really!

Funny bones

Why is a funny bone called a funny bone? It's not funny at all when you bang it is it? In fact, it hurts like hell. I mention funny bones in this book because on holiday you seem to bang your funny bone a lot more than you would do at home. The reason for this is that whilst you are in the UK your elbows are protected by the sleeves of at least one garment and, more often than not, a number of garments such as sweaters, jackets and coats.

On holiday, however, the chances are that you will be walking around all day and evening with exposed elbows. It can happen anywhere. You can be leaning against a bar, resting your elbow on a dining table, turning over on your sun bed, turning around in the shower – bang, 'Ouch, *******!'

Watch your funny bone on holiday because it isn't funny at all!

Funny books

If you read a funny book around the swimming pool or on the beach whilst on holiday, then you are in grave danger making a proper fool of yourself. There you are, reading your funny book and all is quiet around you; you get to a funny bit and it's – 'Phooooooah, ha ha ha - oops!' Everyone else isn't reading your funny book so they look at you as though you have just escaped from somewhere or other. It's now a straight face until you get to the next funny bit then it's – 'Phooooooah, ha ha ha – oops' again!

Miserable nerds, they're probably reading a stamp collectors book or something similar!

G

Game boys and girls

Do children ever speak to their parents and other people these days? Whenever you see any children on holiday with their parents, they inevitably have their heads permanently pressed into a hand held computer of some description or other with their fingers belting hell out of a tiny key pad twenty to the dozen. They haven't got a clue what's going on around them and they are totally disinterested in any kind of conversation whatsoever. However – it's the future, and I bet you rely on these little computer wizards to alter the digital clock on your microwave or TV when the clocks go backwards or forwards. Come on, admit it, you tut at these young people with their heads in a mini computer but you know damn well that you need them badly every Spring and Autumn. Your grand parents probably tutted at you years ago with your stupid hula hoop, plastic Beatles wig or Action Man. It's no different really. Is it?

Gang plank (to the aircraft)

I don't think it's called a gang plank but I don't know the proper name. That long mobile bendy corridor thing that leads from the terminal building onto your aircraft. There are no windows in them until the very last bit where it connects to the plane. The first thing I do when I get to that window, I can't help it, is to look at the aircraft fuselage. I have to see if the aircraft is very new or if it has chipped paint work which means it could be old.

If it's chipped, then it could crash. Couldn't it?

Gap in the queue

Why is everyone so harassed when they are in a check in queue at the airport? If the queue in front of you moves a few inches then you are right up behind the person in front of you, pushing your cases within an inch of their heels. If the queue moves forward slightly but the person directly in front of you doesn't move, then they leave a gap and you get really annoyed don't you? 'They haven't moved and I want to move nearer to the desk – what's wrong with them – aaaaaargh!'

Calm down!

Germolene

Oh Germolene, it's the best medication in the whole world. Take some with you as Germolene can cure anything from a mosquito bite to a hatchet wound if your wife forgets her HRT tablets. As a child my Mum used to put Germolene on just about any kind of ailment you care to name. I seem to remember that it was pink at that time and stained my clothes. As I injured myself virtually every day in one form or another, all my clothes seemed to have pink marks all over them. Its white now, so don't worry about that.

Germolene – put it near the top of your holiday packing list!

Gifts

What an absolute pain in the bottom that is. I think this taking a gift home for every man and his brother thing is dying out a bit now but it still goes on. By all means take a small gift home for children but some people spend half of their holiday shopping for poxy gifts that nobody wants. Who really wants a tacky metal Eiffel Tower, a pink flamenco dancer Barbie type doll, a Fez or a black hairy bull with a sword stuck in it?

They might say 'Thank you' and tell you how nice it is, but they're really thinking to themselves 'That's atrocious, I'll bin it once they've gone'.

Ginger feet

During autumn in Mediterranean holiday resorts, there are millions and millions of oranges growing on trees all over the towns and cities. Nobody picks them and in certain public places it's completely illegal to pick an orange from a tree. What do you get – ginger feet!

Oranges drop off the trees onto the pavements and the roads. They get squashed, and when you then walk (skate) over them in your new flip flops, your feet turn orange. It looks as though your feet have a fantastic tan. I reckon those red, sore, blotchy type people should roll around in the squashed oranges for ten minutes or so and get a free sun tan. Although you may look a bit of a tosspot rolling around on the pavement, your first in a lifetime sun tan will do your street cred' the world of good and its free.

Girly wee

Is it just me? I'm a normal bloke (I think) and when I go for a wee wee then I stand in front of the toilet, pull down the zip of my trousers and perform the task. No problem. However, whilst on holiday and wearing just a pair of shorts or a pair of swim shorts, I seem to go all girly when I go for a wee wee. Instead of doing my normal stand up bit, I automatically pull my shorts down and sit on the toilet like a girly. Why is that?

It's quite common isn't it? Come on guys, tell me it is. Oh hell; everyone's going to take the mickey out of me now!

Go and see the castle

Let's go tomorrow eh?

If you are staying in a Mediterranean coastal holiday resort then it is quite common for there to be a castle within view. I have done it lots of times and I guess you have, 'We'll go up there tomorrow'. You can be sat on the beach within sight of the castle and one of you will almost certainly say something like, 'We must go up and have a look around the castle'.

You never go though; because you can't be bothered!

Go karts

Ooooh – go karts; I love 'em.

I never even think of going to a Go Kart track during the year, but when I go on holiday and see a Go Kart track: that's it! I have to go on the Go Karts and within an instant I get my Nigel Mansell head on. I usually stand there for a while watching the people going round the track at that particular moment and sussing out the form, which is pretty futile really as those people will have come off the track by the time I get on it.

I used to drive around 50,000 miles a year at one point in my life and like to think that I'm a fairly good driver. However, once I get that helmet on and sit in that little cart a couple of inches from the ground, I instantly turn into a complete and utter raving lunatic. The Go Kart track guy starts telling me this and telling me that but I am completely oblivious to anything he says, 'yeah yeah yeah, just get out of the way and let me carve some of those others up'. I don't know why I do it but I just can't help it. I should be banned from Go Kart tracks and actually, I once was.

Quite a few years ago, when I was the Sales Director of one of our group printing companies in Leeds, I decided to have a corporate event for our best customers at a new Go Kart track which had opened near Bradford. Big mistake. We took over the track for an evening and everyone had to go through qualifying events which would eventually finish up with a final. A couple of my sales guys were there, but most of the competitors were our major customers. 'Take it easy Stuart, it's only a game, let the customers win'. Sack that! In the cart I get for the first race and I shot off straight into the lead but destroyed a pile of tyres on the second corner. Spin, screech, off again to carve my way back to the front. I really don't know what happened to me, but I was bashing and banging my best customers all over the track. As far as I was concerned, they were my enemies and I was Mad Max. As I was tearing around the track carving up everyone in sight, I could see the rest of our group stood near the pits with their hands on their heads and their mouths wide open in complete astonishment. I won the race and when I pulled into the pits at the end, two of the track attendants ran over, dragged me out of the Kart, called me every kind of lunatic you can imagine and escorted me to the exit.

'Hang on a minute, what are you doing?'

'Get out, we've had some nutters in here since we opened, but you take the biscuit pal. You're a complete and utter suicide case'.

'I thought I did quite well. I won didn't I?'

'Just get the hell out and don't come back. You need certifying'.

'But it's my event. I organized it'.

'Yes, but you paid in advance so get the hell out and let these other people enjoy themselves'.

That was it. I was kicked out of my own Go Kart event so I had to go across the road to the pub on my own. That's not fair is it?

Go Karts – if you have a high level of competitiveness, double your travel insurance.

Going to the beach

Oh hell. I really really really hate getting all the things together for the beach. Is it just us? All we're going to do is go down to the beach for a spot of sunbathing and possibly a swim but the logistics involved in that are horrendous. If you're a well organized person you will probably have taken a beach bag on holiday with you but it makes no difference because they're never big enough. Towels, books, sun tan creams, personal hi-fi, tissues, bottle of water.

'Have we got everything?'

'I think so'.

'Mobile phones; have you put the mobile phones in?'

'I think so?'

'I best pull all this stuff out and double check – yes, here they are'.

'Reading glasses, have you put those in?'

'I think so?'

By this time you are seriously losing your box. You have the beach bag, bulging shorts pockets and two plastic carrier bags full of all the things you 'think' you might need for the beach. You look like a bunch of gypo's with bad attitude. You're only going about a hundred yards for a few hours but you look as though you're going for three weeks.

'Oh, that was a struggle. Anyway we're here now'.

'Did you pick the money up?'

'Ah poo. I'm not going back there again. I'm going for a pint. Ah double poo, I haven't got any money because we forgot it.'

Slap head!

Graffitti (foreign)

Just like virtually anywhere else in the world, there is graffiti in foreign holiday resorts. The only difference is that you haven't got a clue what it says. No 'El Kilroyo' here! I have seen British tourists walking down streets, looking at a wall full of graffiti and saying something like, 'Oh look, they have graffiti here too'. What they don't know is that the graffiti could well be saying something like, 'Go home English toss pot'. Very nice indeed!

You wouldn't know would you? It's worrying.

Gun and a whistle

Have you seen the foreign policemen? You must have done as they are permanently walking around town, which is one hell of a novelty to British tourists. Brits going abroad find it absolutely fascinating to learn that policemen actually have legs, as all they ever see of British policemen are a pair of shoulders and a head.

The reason for this is that policemen in the UK spend all of their time sat in panda cars with sandwiches, a flask and the heater on full. Foreign policemen however, have a permanent foot presence in towns and cities but their policing type implements are a very strange combination. They always, but always, have a whistle which in many cases is permanently stuck in their mouth and – er – a gun! A gun and a whistle don't seem to go together somehow. Foreign policemen are a bit like urban football referees as any misdemeanor warrants a quick whistle and the culprit immediately toes the line. But he would wouldn't he? No whistle then a yellow card and a booking here. Oh no. First it's the whistle and if you know damn well that Monsieur or Senor Plod has a shooter then you're hardly likely to stick your tongue out at him and shout 'Ner ner sticky bum', are you?

If you hear a whistle whilst on your foreign holiday; just put your arms up in the air – it's safer!

Gun shots

If you hire a car whilst on your foreign holiday and drive up into the mountains, then the chances are that you will hear gun shots. Don't worry, Hitler, Mussolini or Franco haven't come back. Many foreigners who live in the country go out and shoot rabbits. If you live in the countryside and fancy a rabbit for your tea then fair enough, shoot one. Some of these guys, however, go mental and it sounds like a war. They waste loads and loads of poor little bunny's for no apparent reason as they can't eat them all - can they?

Remember: the next time one of your children or grand children says to you, 'Was Wodger Wabbit a weal wabbit and who killed Wodger Wabbit?' You say, 'That nasty foreign man in the hills with a big gun'. He's a cruel *******!

Guttering

There isn't any!

When you go on holiday abroad you should always buy a surf

board to put on your head if it rains. When it rains abroad, it really rains and the buildings don't have any guttering. Why is that? Surely guttering isn't a recent invention is it? I've never seen it on Tomorrows World –

'Here, tonight, exclusively, we have for you the latest in building technology: GUTTERING!'

You can be walking along the seafront at most foreign holiday resorts when it's raining and there's Niagara Falls coming down from every shop front on the promenade.

'El Gutteringo' as the Spanish would call it – if they had any!

H

Harbours and Marinas

What exactly is the difference between a harbour and a marina? Is it that a harbour is a harbour but if it's in a posh place then it's called a marina? If so, who exactly is it who decides what is a posh place and what isn't? Whilst on holiday you will often hear people saying 'I think we'll just go for a walk around the harbour today' or 'I think we'll just go for a walk around the marina today'. You wouldn't think anything at all about either of those comments, but just think about it. When is a harbour a harbour and when is it a marina?

Anyway; now that we haven't sorted that one out - I love walking around these places gawping at the beautiful yachts. Who owns them? Is there so much money in the whole world? You can go to places like St. Tropez on the French Riviera or Puerto Banus on the Costa del Sol and see so called yachts which are more like ships than yachts. They're absolutely huge and sometimes have people sat on the back with a bottle of champagne and a plateful of canapés posing for all the passers by and who the hell can blame them? If you stand there looking at these beautiful mega expensive vessels for a while, you should take note of the comments coming out of the mouths of other fellow gawpers. The diversity of conversation is absolutely fascinating with such things as –

1. 'Look at this one – wow!'
2. 'I wonder how much that one cost. What do you think?'

3. 'Wouldn't it be great to have a look around one of these?'

4. 'What kind of person could afford that thing?'

5. 'I wish we could have one of those don't you?'

6. 'I couldn't even afford one of those jet skis hanging off the back!'

7. 'I bet the owner's a drugs dealer.'

8. 'They may have pots and pots of money but I bet they're not happy.'

9. 'Look at that big fat rich greedy ******* sat there with a bottle of champagne.' (Just a touch of jealousy there I think).

Go to the harbour to look at the fishing boats, but go to the marina if you really want to be jealous!

'Have we got more left than we've had?'

It's crazy really but Chris always says this to me whilst we are on holiday, 'Have we got more left than we've had?' It only comes out about three days into our two week holiday, but once it's said for the first time, I know damn well that she will say it every day afterwards until the eighth day and then I get scared. Instead of 'Yes', it's going to be 'No' today. Will the question come during the morning or during the afternoon? Here it comes 'Have we got more left than we've already had?' 'Er - - er - - no.' Then I leg it to the nearest bar because I know she will start sulking!

Does your wife do that? Why can't women work it out for themselves as it would save all that mooching about on the eighth day and thereafter!

Head phones on the plane

If you want to make a complete plant pot of yourself on the plane then get a set of headphones and watch a film or listen to the radio. It has me in stitches. Everyone is sat there on the plane minding their own business when someone pipes up at the top of their voice 'WHAT TIME IS IT' or "I HOPE THE WEATHER'S HOT WHEN WE GET THERE'. They're shouting at the top of their voice and their partner looks acutely embarrassed and goes bright red. They then dig this shouting type person in the ribs and tell them to 'Shut up!' They've had the volume up high and therefore speak accordingly (I think?)

Phooooh, ha ha – what a nutter!

High balconies

'Oh no - I'm not going out there!'

It is a fact of life that many men are seriously poo your pants frightened of heights and I freely admit that I'm one of them. I don't know why it is, but it appears to me that heights present a far greater fear to men than they do to women. Why is that?

Chris and I once arrived at our very nice Spanish hotel and were given the keys to a room on what seemed like the one hundred and eighty fourth floor (I think it was actually the tenth). As soon as I walked in the front door and towards the balcony I had to sit down on the couch immediately as I turned all dizzy and girly like -'Oooh, the buildings moving and I'm going to fall out'. We tried to change our room but couldn't as the hotel was full and the holiday rep obviously thought that I was just a bit of a wuss. I swear I never went out onto that balcony once and spent the whole fortnight listening for earthquakes.

That's normal isn't it?

Home made frozen food

A lot of people choose to stay in apartments rather than hotels in order to do their own thing and not be handcuffed by set meal times. Many of these people who stay in apartments never even think of using the cooking facilities, preferring to eat out all of the time. There are, however, people who only eat out some of the time but also like to have a nice meal in their apartment some evenings. Chris and I fell into this bracket when we went on holiday from the UK. One thing you should never do is the thing most of us do at home – freeze the bits that are left over. You are only here for a week or two. You make a nice spag' bol' and enjoy every mouthful on your balcony with a bottle of wine or ten. There's some food left over – it's a shame to waste it. You then put it into some receptacle or other and hide it in the ice cube box in the fridge. Who the hell are you kidding? Are you really going to eat that before you go home? No! Do you really believe that the nice foreign cleaning lady is going to take it home and give it to her kids?

Hormone soup

You always get the family on holiday who have a pubescent kid don't you? It can be a boy or a girl, it doesn't matter. Thirteen or fourteen years old with a face looking like a pizza because they have serious acne. They're too young to go out to the pub drinking and yet they think they're too old to play with the other kids. They're in the middle, so what do they do – sulk! Their body is just a soup of hormones and they can't quite decide who they are. Are they big people, or are they still little people? Slouching in a chair, waving their legs around and looking at everyone else including their own parents as if they're an offence to them.

'Would you like a drink?' - 'I don't know'.

'Where would you like to go today?' – 'I don't know'.

'What's your name?' – 'I don't know'.

'Do you know anything?' – 'I don't know'.

For Christ's sake, give your head a shake!

Hotel bars

I really cannot understand the mentality of hotel managers abroad. If drinks in hotel bars were a bit more expensive than the bars outside then most people wouldn't object. They would be prepared to pay a slightly higher price in order to stay in the comfort of their hotel. Most hotels however, take the p**s. Many hotel bars charge treble the going rate. They then have the nerve to have a happy hour when drinks are 'Half price'. Half of what price? These half price drinks are still more expensive than they are outside and the hotel manager thinks he's doing you a favour. They should call it the MISERABLE HOUR! Don't stand for it, get your own back. Sneak a load of beer tinnies into your hotel room, pinch a towel - oh, you already have done – that's all right then! Also, there appears to be no middle diddle with hotel bars. They are either completely over the top pretentious with no atmosphere whatsoever or they are complete dumps with tatty ping pong tables, fruit machines and hoards of kids running wild all around the place. I don't think I have ever seen a 'Proper' pub type bar in a foreign hotel!

I wonder why tourists go outside to drink?

Hotel lifts

Be patient, you're on holiday, there's no rush. Yes there is. Where's the lift? Whichever floor you are on except the lobby, you can wait for fifteen years for a lift. You can go up to your room because you have forgotten something; you're only in there for about twenty seconds and when you get back to the lift – it's gone! Even in the middle of the night; it doesn't stay until someone on another floor presses the button, it just goes. Where does it go to? You can wait forever and wish that you had brought some sandwiches when all of a sudden the light comes on and it's a sigh of relief – 'Hah – the lift's here.' The door then opens and the lift is full of other people – 'Aaaargh!' I bet they haven't been waiting for half as long as you have, it's not fair! Sack that; run down ten flights of stairs or slide down the banister if there is one and pretend that you've run out of toilet paper.

People who won't use lifts don't know how lucky they are, their stress levels must be half of everyone else's.

Having said that, how on earth do these people cope whilst on holiday if they get put on the fourteenth floor? I think it is highly unlikely that all the people in the world who won't use lifts are super fit and think nothing of jogging up and down fourteen flights of steps. I am sure that they request a low level floor when they book their holidays but let's face it; most holiday reps don't even look at the special requests and even if they do, it's too much trouble.

Someone once suggested to me that if you were in a lift and it broke (as in started dropping to the ground floor at tremendous velocity), then all you have to do is jump up and down. This person reckoned that you then had a 50/50 chance of survival. 'Oh yeah, right, how's that then?' He claimed that as long as the lift hit the ground whilst you were in the 'up' part of the jump, then you would come down as safely as if you had just jumped off the floor. You may be surprised to hear that this conversation took place in a pub! However, this person seems not to have taken into consideration the fact that you would already be travelling downwards at tremendous speed and therefore would still get splattered whether you were playing jump or not.

So: If you were frightened of lifts before, then I should remain frightened of them if I were you because my friend doesn't know what the hell he's talking about.

Hotel patio doors

Foreign glass cleaner must surely be the best in the world. You must have done it at least once. You get the key to your room, walk in and say 'Wow, look at that view'. You then walk towards the balcony and BANG – 'Aaaaaargh, *******, I think I've broken my nose'. The patio door's closed but it looks open because you can't see it.

Let's all play nut the door - again!

Hotel receptionists

Why do most hotel receptionists abroad appear to be blind?

You can go to many, if not most foreign hotel reception desks and the receptionist just ignores you. You know they have seen you but they just ignore you. It infuriates me. You have paid good money for your holiday and it's you who keeps this supercilious twonker in a job. Anyone would think he was on a higher plane than us mere mortals but what is he? A receptionist - which is a bit of a Jessy's job anyway!

Chris and I were once staying in a Paris hotel and I swear I thought I had turned invisible. Other people must have noticed me as nobody bumped into me. Not this tupenny 'I've got a brass tie pin' receptionist girly type guy; he just ignored me. Not once, but every time I went to reception. We were in the bar one evening and I said to Chris –

'Go and ask that guy on reception for a long stand'.

'What?' she said.

'Go and ask that receptionist guy for a long stand'.

'What are you on about, what's a long stand?'

'It's the only thing you can get at that reception'.

I didn't like that guy!

Hotel room (yours)

How many times have you arrived at your hotel or apartment block and been really pleased with your room, or at least well satisfied. UNTIL THE SECOND OR THIRD DAY! You are happy with what you have been given until you notice someone in another room who gets the sun early evening on their balcony which is the time you would prefer it. It may be that your sea view appeared to be good when you arrived but you got talking to someone in the bar who showed you their room and the sea view is better than yours. That's it; the lip's out isn't it? You're now telling everyone you meet that the hotel is naff, the room is naff, and to rub salt into the wounds, you also tell them that the food is naff. Why? Because someone got a better room than yours - Didums!

Hotel sun beds

Are there enough to go round? Yes usually. Then why the hell do people set their alarm clocks and go down to the hotel pool in order to put towels on sun beds? I'll tell you why. It's because they want THAT one. Not another one – THAT one! What's so special about THAT particular sun bed then? The only logical reason I can think of for this strange pastime is that these alarm clock type people are those who have frequented working men's clubs for most of their lives. 'That's MY chair - I sit THERE, my dad before me sat THERE, and his dad before him sat THERE – so THERE – ner ner ner'.

Go boil your head!

Hypnotists

How do they do all that stuff? I have to admit that I used to be a serious sceptic of the holiday bar hypnotist. I just assumed that they had ringers in the audience and that it was all a huge con. A few years ago in Tenerife, Chris and I went to see one of these hypnotists and just for a laugh we went up onto the stage as volunteers. There were flashing coloured strobe lights and this guy asked us all to squeeze our hands together and then squeeze them tighter and tighter until we couldn't pull them apart. There was no doubt about it, my hands were starting to stick together so I loosened them and didn't go under – Chris did though! The hypnotist came along the line of volunteers and sent back to their seats about half of us who hadn't succumbed to his spell.

Chris is a fairly quiet person and there is no way on Gods earth that she would do anything out of the ordinary in front of an audience, but there she was, pretending to be a ballet dancer and sat in a seat totally convinced by this guy that she was on a plane which was about to crash. He had these people doing all kinds of things and Chris was one of them. This convinced me beyond any doubt whatsoever that they were genuinely under the spell of the guy.

Half way through the show there was a break and the hypnotist said to Chris and the other guzunders, 'I am going to wake you up now and you will enjoy the break with the rest of the audience. However, when I say the word (I think it was plums but it doesn't matter) you will wave your arms around in the air, start shouting and enthusiastically run back onto the stage'. He clicked his fingers and the guzunders came round immediately promptly returning to their seats for the break. Chris was perfectly normal but didn't have a clue what had been going on. We went to the bar and had a drink. Sure enough, a few minutes later the hypnotist shouted over the microphone 'Plums'. I couldn't believe it, Chris went mental waving her arms around, shouting and then ran back down to the stage. I stood there with my mouth open – she doesn't do things like that! Off he goes again, getting these people doing all kinds of stupid things and then at the end of the show he got this lady to lay, face up, across four bar stools. He kept asking her to get stiffer and stiffer and then took one of the centre stools away. Stiffer and stiffer, he then took the other centre bar stool away. This lady had the back of her head on one stool and the heels of her feet on the other with only fresh air in the middle. Now that is impossible for anyone to do. I don't care if you are the fittest person alive or if you have a broom handle stuck up your bottom, it can't be done. I saw it, honest, with my own eyes, she was suspended in mid air and I had seen the same lady around our hotel swimming pool a few times prior to this event. She was a tourist, not a ringer. How do they do all that? It's absolutely amazing.

Once the show was over and Chris returned to her seat, she said that she had a horrific headache so I went over to the hypnotist and told him about the problem. He immediately came over to Chris, put his hand on her forehead, clicked his fingers and said 'Sleep'. Bang: she had gone under again. He told her that when he clicked his fingers again she would wake up and the headache would have disappeared. It had – she was perfectly alright and the headache had cleared completely. A sceptic no longer, that's a real talent.

Whilst finishing our drinks we got talking to the hypnotist and I suggested to him that he must be able to do virtually anything he wanted with his powers. He was adamant that although he can get people to do all kinds of silly things he cannot get people (women) to do something they don't want to do – yea right! You could offer to pay Chris ten thousand pounds and she wouldn't do that silly stuff in front of an audience unless she was hypnotized. She just wouldn't do it, she wouldn't want to. I guess that blows his argument out of the water so just remember – never go on a date with a hypnotist and never ever go back to his place.

You could be doing some really unnatural things without knowing anything about it!

I

I bet you

Whilst on the beach you will often just sit there having a skeg at everyone else on the beach. You will be glancing around and then all of a sudden your eyes will stop at a man or a lady stood perfectly still in the sea submerged up to about waist height. You will watch them for thirty seconds or so and they don't move, 'Mmmmmmm?' They're having a wee wee in the sea.

I bet you; any money you want!

I could get used to this!

Have you ever said that? I bet you a squillion pounds that you have; everyone has. On the first day of your holiday you are sat in a bar overlooking the sea and you say 'Ah, I could get used to this'. Out of all the things you could say in those circumstances, you always say that – why?

I haven't got any spending money left!

'I spent it all in the airport with my mates. We had a long delay and all I had were eighteen Jack Daniels and cokes at thirty two pounds a time, plus a breakfast which was (I think) about one hundred and two pounds. I then bought some perfume, after shave lotion, an inflatable aircraft and some Speedo swimming trunks in order to pose for the ladies. I don't know where all my spending money has gone.'

'Oh hell; I wish I was good with money like my (ex) wife was!'

Ice creams

There are few things more refreshing than an ice cream on the beach during your summer holiday. The only problem is that us Brits are not used to eating ice creams in the baking heat and if you're not careful then you can look like a proper 100% dip stick. You take the wrapper off your ice cream and before you know what's happening its melting at tremendous speed, so you start eating it as quickly as possible in order not to waste any. First it's ice cream running down your chin and then it's dripping from both the ice cream and your chin onto your chest and you look like a baby after its first bottle.

'Slobber slobber, suck suck; ah Christ. I knew I should have just got a pint!'

Ice cube trays (foreign)

If you want to use the ice cube tray in your foreign apartment or hotel room (if you have a fridge) then you would be well advised to bring a hammer and chisel with you. Foreign ice cube trays are the most frustrating stupid things imaginable. The plastic is so thick that you can't bend them so you have to run them underneath the hot water tap in order to release the cubes. The problem is that the cubes are so small that all you finish up with is hot water, which is not a lot of good in your gin and tonic is it?

Warm gin and tonic? Yuk!

Idiots

Just like anywhere else in the world there are plenty of complete idiots in foreign holiday resorts. Most of them are British ex pats and they live there permanently. 'National Talking Rubbish Day' was invented by ex pats. In fact National Talking Rubbish Day is every day in many of the British pubs in foreign holiday resorts. Where do they get their money from – I don't know? They appear to be on permanent holiday as many don't work. They just have enough money on them to get completely legless and then have more money the next day to get completely legless again, it's a mystery.

I live in Spain and I don't do that. Am I doing something wrong?

'I'll just stay a little longer love if that's okay?'

We have all done this guys haven't we? You're having a great time and it would be fair to say that you are just a little bit hammered. Your wife doesn't realize that you are as hammered as you really are because you're trying very hard to be a really good boy. She wants to go back to the hotel but you want to stay a lot longer. 'I'll just stay a little longer love if that's okay?' You have been good and as you have asked in a really nice way then she agrees as long as you don't stay very long. 'Of course not, I'll just have a nightcap'. That's it, you're on one and you get completely legless because you're on holiday. One hour, two hours and it's the old 'I might as well get hung for a sheep as a lamb'. Next morning (or afternoon depending on when you come round), you're in big trouble. It's always the same question, before you have even looked her in the eyes, 'Where were you last night?'

Remember this: your answer should always be 'There you go, bringing up the past again!' Then start sulking, it always works. So I am told!

'I'm missing our dog'

If you get talking to a fellow holiday maker, it invariably starts with something along the lines of 'Have you been here before' or 'Which hotel are you staying in'. It can then develop into all kinds of conversations about the weather, where you come from, or which excursions you have booked. Once the conversation has progressed beyond this introductory stage someone will almost certainly come out with 'I miss our dog'. Oh, okay then.

No mention of the children or grand children – they miss a dog!

Implants

It's not unusual these days to see women in the UK who have obviously had breast implants. When you're on the beach abroad however – well – they're just there, aren't they? It's a strange thing this; but men just can't help looking at women's breasts especially if they aren't covered up on the beach and it can cause serious arguments. These huge cantilevered implant thingies are fine and if women want to have them then what the hell is wrong with that. I'll tell you what's wrong with that. Other women don't like them. Why? Is it jealousy, is it envy, is it the fact that their husband keeps staring at them completely mesmerized by the fact that they stick straight up into the air when the woman is actually lying down horizontally on her sun bed?

Men get seriously told off for looking at them, even if they try to be subtle through some of those mirror type sunglasses. Women can be quite bitchy towards the implant lady and come out with all kinds of remarks such as 'They look ridiculous' or 'Anyone could have some of those, even you if you wanted some'. I even once heard a woman referring to another lady's implants as 'She's got some of those bought t*ts'. Now come on ladies, let's just think about these remarks –

'They look ridiculous'. If you think they look ridiculous then you must have been looking at them yourself, so why are you playing hell with your husband for looking. What's the difference?

'Anyone could have some of those, even you if you wanted some'. I don't think so do you? Can you imagine the husband turning round to the lady one day and saying something like 'I think I'll book myself into the clinic for a pair of those false breasts'. That's instant divorce stuff isn't it?

'She's got some of those bought t*ts'. That's just rough and I detect just the slightest hint of bitchiness there don't you?

Breast implants – Be damned and have a look. Most people find them bloody fascinating!

Inflatables

Abroad, you can get inflatable whatever you wants (see also li-lo's). There are the standard air beds in every colour and pattern you can imagine and then there are the other inflatables such as crocodiles, dolphins, ducks, whales, rubber rings printed to look like a Michelin tyre, inflatable arm chairs with a little slot to put your drink in and many many more. But then, oh then, we have – oh yes - INFLATABLE GUITARS! That's right – inflatable guitars! Why, in the name of God would anyone want to own an inflatable guitar? These inflatable guitars are life size guitars printed on the front to look like one of those pop group type electric guitars. They obviously have no strings so you can't play a tune on them and they are the same size as a proper guitar so you can't float on it either.

Why, oh why pray tell me, would anyone go into a shop and buy an inflatable guitar? It's just not right is it?

Come on; would you buy an inflatable guitar? You would! Oh, okay then, it must just be me!

Inflation

There has been inflation over the years abroad just as there has been inflation in the UK. Also, prices have gone up significantly in real terms within the Eurozone since the introduction of the euro. Some tourists, particularly older ones, don't appear to realize this. You can almost guarantee that you will get talking to an older couple on your foreign holiday or they will get talking to you and they will come out with a ridiculous statement along the lines of - 'Things have gone up here haven't they? When we were in Benidorm in 1977 the prices were a lot cheaper'.

Well they would have been wouldn't they?

Instant dislike

One thing that most people don't even consider is the fact that whilst at home in the UK they are usually surrounded by people who they know whether it be family, friends, neighbours or colleagues. Whilst on holiday however, all the people you see and meet are complete and utter strangers. It's a strange thing but when you are thrown into a situation where you don't know anyone, you tend to eye all your fellow holiday makers up and make first impressions –

'He looks a bit shady'.

'That couple over there are always p****d'.

'I wish they would sort that child out because he's doing my head in'.

'She looks a bit like Susan Soandso from the newsagents'.

'He looks a lot older than she does; I bet she's after his money'.

You don't even know these people, but it's a perfectly normal human thing to do – I think?

Internet Cafes

What possesses people to go into Internet cafes whilst on holiday? They come away on holiday to relax and get away from the day to day British rat race and what do they do? They go into an Internet café in order to catch up on their e-mails. Are they mad? Some people even go in to surf the Internet when they could and should be sat on the beach or in a bar, or both. 'Ask Jeeves' – who is this Jeeves anyway? He claims to know everything but nobody seems to know him. Where does he live? If he's so clever how come he doesn't appear on all the quiz programmes and win every week? Who wants to be a millionaire? Jeeves does. He wouldn't have to sit in his dingy office answering stupid questions all the time then would he?

Ironing before you pack

Why bother? Most women go to a lot of trouble ironing all their husbands' holiday clothes and then packing them neatly in his case for him. What does the man do an hour prior to leaving the house? He remembers all the little things that he likes to shove into the case himself so he just lifts up the nicely folded shirts and bungs the lot in. Once you arrive at the hotel your husband opens his case and doesn't want to criticize the standard of your ironing but he's certainly not over impressed. He genuinely thinks that you're rubbish at ironing and never even considers the fact that it is him who has creased everything.

Ironmongers shops

Ladies; if your husband or partner disappears for an hour on holiday, you shouldn't just assume that he has gone to a bar because blokes love wandering around foreign ironmongers shops; they're great. The old ironmonger's shop in the UK has all but disappeared to be taken over by huge DIY stores. Not abroad. They're fantastic and sell all the things that most guys love messing about with. There are baskets full of spanners, nuts, bolts, hammers and all that stuff. I don't know why we do it, especially on holiday, because let's face it you're not likely to buy a lump hammer and take it home with you – are you? Even if you did buy a lump hammer, you would have some serious explaining to do with the customs boys. That's not the point; we men love wandering around looking at all that old 'keep it in the garden shed stuff'. Some of these ironmongers shops even sell huge knifes and swords. Seriously, you can walk in and buy a huge pirate type proper sword then walk around pretending to be a proper pirate.

I don't think that you would get very far if you didn't have it in a bag though?

'Is all my stuff in the suitcase?'

What is 'stuff?' I use the statement 'Is all my stuff in the suitcase' as an example of this strange word because it is only one of literally thousands of statements containing the word 'Stuff'. 'Stuff' must surely be one of the most common everyday words in the whole of the English language but it doesn't actually mean anything does it? I bet you use the word 'Stuff' lots and lots of times every day in all kinds of situations, I know I do, but just have a think about it. What does it mean?

'Is all my stuff in the suitcase?'   What stuff?

'I don't know why we brought all this stuff?'   What stuff?

'Have you read that – I can't understand all that stuff?'   What stuff?

'Where have you put all of my stuff?'   What stuff?

'I'd better nip down to the shop for some stuff.'   What stuff?

'Did we bring any sun tan stuff?'   What stuff?

'There's lots of stuff in this kitchen cupboard.'   What stuff?

You see – what stuff – what is this word 'stuff?'

'Is it hot enough for you then?'

How many times do you get asked that question on your holiday? It can be anyone; someone staying in your hotel, someone you get talking to on the beach or around the pool, or even a total stranger that you have never clapped eyes on in your whole life before. 'Is it hot enough for you then?' What sort of question is that? The heat is probably burning you like hell and you are a bit hot and bothered so the last thing you want is some strange person asking if it's hot enough for you.

Tell them that if they can't think of anything original to say then they should keep their mouth shut.

Is there enough room on the beach?

If you go to a foreign tourist resort during the month of August then you had better get down onto the beach early. Most foreign families take their annual holiday during August and many of them for the whole of August. Us Brits usually take to the beach a standard issue beach towel and a bag with our other bits in. Not the foreigners; they appear to take the whole contents of their house. First, the tent comes out and if you watch them they don't even have half a clue how to erect the damn thing. Two hours later and they start walking backwards and forwards to their cars and vans like ants bringing all their other stuff (there's that word 'stuff' again) to the tent. It fascinates me! They bring armchairs, tables, dining chairs and I once saw a Greek family struggling down the beach from their van with a huge wooden bureau! Why on earth would anyone want to take a huge wooden bureau down to the beach with them unless the family fortune was hidden in it and they daren't leave it at home – it's not logical?

Watch out for foreign families on the beach during August; they take the lot and there's hardly room for anyone else.

'It's the worst place I've ever been to!'

I've done it myself. If you go on your hard earned holiday and you get bad weather, the chances are that you will go back home and tell everyone what a crap place so and so is. I once went to Calella in Spain and it rained just about every day. I now hate the place and wouldn't go back there even if it was completely free of charge.

What is there to do in a foreign holiday resort when it's lashing it down with rain? You could go out for a walk (slalom) in your shorts and flip flops or you could just stay in the hotel bar and get yourself legless. It may come as a surprise to you, but many Brits appear to go for option number two. The result is a hotel bar and lobby which resembles a refugee camp. All the Brits are there off their trolleys and there are screaming kids running riot through the lobby and down the corridors. Every two minutes you will hear someone say 'I hope it's okay tomorrow', but it isn't. 'Oh hell, I hate this place, what a complete dump'. You've had a completely naff holiday and when you get back to the UK you're telling everyone who will listen that it's the worst holiday you've ever had and what a dump the resort was.

It's not the resorts fault that it rained for the duration of your holiday and if you returned when the sun was shining, then the chances are that you would think it was great. Still: it was raining so the resort's a crap hole, okay!

J

Jalking

Thankfully, most people are sensible enough not to go jogging in the blistering heat on holiday (see also Jogging). There are, however, people who go out thinking they're jogging when they are in fact, not really jogging at all. What on earth are they doing? It's not quite a walk and it's not quite a jog. It's sort of the movement of a jogger but at the speed of a walk. It's a new hybrid sports pastime which falls somewhere between walking and jogging. It is performed by people who are not fit enough to jog properly and they are prime candidates to be laughed at.

Jam portions (foreign)

What is it? It looks like a jam portion and it has a picture of a strawberry or an apricot on the top. Once you open it, it looks like jam(ish). You then dip your knife in and spread it on your toast prior to having a bite. In the mouth it goes and it tastes like – erm – erm – well – nothing actually!

Jelly fish

Be careful when you go into the sea abroad, very careful indeed. You can go for weeks and not see a single jelly fish in the sea. Then all of a sudden they appear; thousands and thousands of them. If one of those Mediterranean type jelly fish stings you then you'll know about it – it hurts like hell. Many beaches in the

101

major holiday resorts have a first aid hut and many of the staff speak English. If a jelly fish gets you, then leg it to the first aid hut as quickly as you can. Failing that, get yourself to a Chemist shop.

One day, when we had our tea shop in Fuengirola, a guy legged it onto the terrace waving his arms around ferociously and shouting. (Please excuse the language, it's him not me). He came running towards me shouting '******* hell, I don't know what to do, ****, the ********* thing – ouch - *******'. We had customers in at the time and my first reaction was to throw him out but something must be wrong with him surely; nobody normal does this, do they? Could he have that Tourette's syndrome I wondered? I had seen some of these poor people on the TV and they can't help swearing, it's a genuine illness. Calm down, I said to him. 'Calm down, calm ******* down, **** me, the ****'. Right that's it – 'Just shut the **** up', I said (hang on, is this contagious?) 'Oh ****, oh ****, look at this ******* thing'. He then rolled his swim shorts leg up and there was this horrific red rash thing. I thought to myself; surely he can't be so unlucky as to have Tourette's Syndrome AND a sexually transmitted disease as well – can he?

Jelly fish, watch out for them - they make you swear a lot!

Jelly soldier

This is a very strange phenomenon and you have possibly never noticed. Younger men wear long shorts and older men wear short shorts. There is definitely a generation divide when it comes to men's shorts on holiday. I think it must be relevant to fashion eras. When the older men were younger, short shorts were fashionable and these people have never got out of the time warp. Longer shorts then came into fashion but some older men prefer to stay with the short shorts because that's what they have always worn. The problem comes into play when these older men go on holiday because some of them don't wear underpants. I am not trying to say that this is a regular sight but at some point I'm sure that you must have seen it. You can be sat in a bar or a restaurant opposite the 'older guy' when all of a sudden your eyes wander to his shorts and there it is – the little jelly soldier – 'Yuk yuk yuk blaaaah!'

Long shorts should be compulsory!

Jimmy's found a friend

Young children can sometimes be a complete pain on holiday, particularly if they're an only child. You're usually okay for the first day or two, and then you begin to see a bit of boredom creeping in. Let's face it, generally speaking, us adults like nothing more than sitting on the beach sunbathing and generally doing – er – absolutely nothing actually. You can keep a young child amused for a certain amount of time but there are only so many sandcastles you can build. You hope to God that little Jimmy will find a friend on the beach and you will do almost anything to get him (or her) off with a friend or two.

What usually happens is that after a few days you try to coax little Jimmy to make friends with that little boy over there that you've seen on the beach for the last couple of days but it's proving quite difficult to get them off together. You try inviting the other child over to join in your sandcastle building or your football game but sometimes children can play hard to get. There's nothing else for it but to sidle over to the parents and get talking to them in the hope that together, you can get the friendship kicked off. After all, it's in the interest of both sets of parents to have a little peace and quiet whilst the children play amongst themselves. It can sometimes be very frustrating and demoralizing though!

You have tried going down the bringing the children together route, and now you're over there talking to the parents. It seems to be working as sure enough, the children are now chatting away and hopefully that's it for the next week or so. A new found friend, which will make everyone's life so much easier. What happens next?

'Oh I'm so glad that our Jimmy has made friends with your little boy, they seem to be playing so well together now'.

'Yes' says the other little boys mother. 'It's just a shame that they didn't get together earlier because we're going home tomorrow'.

'Whaaaaaaaaat!'

Job

Have you got one? If you are below retirement age and don't have a job then why are you going on holiday in the first place. Why should other people pay for your holiday?

I'm only having a laugh - honest!

Jogging

In one hundred degrees; I don't think so!

Come on, is it me, am I being unfair or am I just simply missing something? Jogging is a very popular pastime and fair play to anyone who enjoys it, but to go jogging on your foreign holiday in the middle of summer can't be good for you - can it? I suppose some people who are good at jogging and take part in marathons etc. have to keep training come what may, and although it doesn't seem to be a particularly good idea to go jogging in the baking hot sunshine, they have to keep their hand in I guess. These slim, nimble marathon type people are not the ones I am talking about, because you must have also seen the fat, middle aged to old jogging type people trying to run along the sea front wearing a head band and looking as if they're about to expire. The reason they look as if they're about to expire is because they are about to expire. It's serious suicide stuff! For a start, they're not running at all, it's more like a forced fast walk (jalking) and sweat is pumping out of them at a frightening rate. They look like a spitting image puppet with water spraying out of every orifice in their body and they're what you might call 'clonked'.

It's just not right – is it?

K

Karaoke

I could probably write a whole book about the different types of Karaoke singers, but most of them are so bad that it would be a total waste time and effort. Foreign Karaoke is no different from Karaoke in the UK I guess, apart from the fact that there are sometimes foreign people taking part and the Brits taking part are even more smashed than they are whilst performing Karaoke at home in the UK.

You have to give it to them; some of these Karaoke singers are good, very good indeed – but not many! Let's have a look at the typical stereotype Karaoke singers.

Elvis – He's got to be there hasn't he? I reckon that nearly half of the men who get up on the holiday Karaoke stage sing an Elvis song. Some of them get completely carried away and really believe that for three minutes or so they are Elvis Presley. The more smashed they are, the more they get carried away, and the more carried away they get, the worse they sound. The top lip's quivering, the legs are shaking, the microphone is half way up his nose and his arms are flying all over the place. From a distance he looks as though he's been plugged into the electricity supply, but in the cold light of day he usually sounds absolutely atrocious!

Gloria Gaynor - That's usually a slapper who has just split up with her boyfriend. She's wrecked, been crying, and hasn't got a clue what the words to the song are apart from 'I "sob" will "sob" survive', whilst at the same time thinking what a complete ******* her (ex) boyfriend is.

Scotsmen – Here he comes; the young Scotsman walking towards the stage like a hermit crab. You know for a cast iron fact which song the drunken Scotsman is going to sing before he even opens his mouth – The Proclaimers! The music begins and he starts singing which isn't too bad, and then here comes the chorus – 'I would walk five hundred miles and then I'd walk five hundred more.' That's it; the feet are stomping as though he's on a parade ground and he's yomping ferociously on the spot. Here we go again - 'I would walk five hundred miles and then I'd walk five hundred more' – he's stomping away and actually believes now that he's wearing hiking boots instead of flip flops. You've seen him; you must have done. He's a clown short of a full circus!

Frank Sinatra – This is usually the older guy who just wants a relaxing sing song and why not? Why not indeed; unless of course the Frank Sinatra song he chooses is New York, New York. Oh no, you know damn well that when that bit towards the end arrives, he will try and do a Can Can impersonation by kicking his stupid legs out in front of him and nearly fall over. If he's lucky enough not to fall over, then he will certainly at least go some way towards spraining his lairum (whatever that is). Here it comes now - 'New Yooork, Nehew Yooooork.' Yeah okay, just get the hell back to your seat mate!

Simply the best – (see Gloria Gaynor) Same slapper but not yet split from her boyfriend!

Like a virgin – Like a what - yeah right! Why do girls and women who look more like an employee from the local rub and tug shop sing a song called 'Like a virgin?' Who do they think they're kidding?

Air guitars – This is often performed to 'We are the champions' by Queen, but it can also be seen accompanying many other rock records on the holiday karaoke. The guy with the air guitar can be a young man, a middle aged man or even some old gimmer. He's got a make believe guitar and he thinks he can play it better than Jimmy Hendrix. What a nutter!

Karaoke kids – I'll finish off with this one because out of all the atrocious karaoke singers in the world, young children are by far the worst. I'm going to be controversial here, again! I don't think children should be allowed to sing on karaoke unless it's a special karaoke for kids. They scream, shout and do your bloody head in. Their parents are sat there smiling, laughing, looking on longingly and saying things like 'Oh isn't he good' or 'She's always been quite musically minded you know'. Everyone else on the other hand is cringing and trying to drink their drink as soon as humanly possible in order to escape the utter purgatory.

Karaoke kids – gag em!

Kites

I wish I could fly a kite. I have to say that throughout any year, I never even think about kites once until I go abroad on holiday. There they are on the beach; people flying kites and I want to do it. I have tried it many times when my son Oliver was younger. There I would be on the beach on the first day of my holiday and inevitably there would be at least one other father flying a kite with his son or daughter. Down to the nearest gift shop I would go like a kid going to buy his first bike and I would buy the biggest daftest kite in the shop. Now, I am worse than useless when it comes to DIY type activities, and one thing I never do is read assembly instructions. 'Oh no, that's not necessary. Printed instructions are only the manufacturers opinion as to how you should assemble it and I know better. I don't need those'. Where kites are concerned, I usually finish up with something which resembles a pile of old fish bones. Buying the biggest most stupid kite in the shop doesn't help either, because you need a degree in order to assemble it. So, it's a bit of huffing, a bit of puffing, a couple of swear words and then off to the beach bar to calm down a bit. Usually, by the time I had got back to my sun bed, Oliver had assembled it perfectly. 'Off we go then. Pheeew, chuckle chuckle, look at those rubbish kites over there son, they're not as good as our big daft Dracula type kite are they? Okay, you're not big enough to launch this kite so I'll have to do it'. 'Oh Dad, you always say that; why can't I launch it?' 'No, no, I'll get it into the air and then I'll hand it over to you and just watch those other Dads faces when they see this thing'. Off I go, legging it down the beach destroying everything and everyone in my path. I'm running like hell forwards but I'm looking up in the air with my arm held high holding onto Count Dracula – not a good combination. Let it go, fall over – clunk, nothing. Up I get, off I go again and it's into a serious run now. Let it go, fall over a sun bed – clunk, nothing.

'Oh sack that son. There must be something wrong with it; the aerodynamics are all wrong'. 'But Dad, it's broken. You've smashed it'. 'No, that wasn't me son. I used to be an expert at flying kites when I was your age. It must be the way you assembled it. I told you to wait until I got back from the beach bar – hic'.

I can't do kites!

L

Ladies - how many times do you pack your cases?

Come on, be honest! Why do you do that – start packing your cases two weeks before you are due to go on holiday and then pack them again – and then again – and then again – and then again? It's not just your case either is it? You pack your husbands case seven times, your children's case nine times and then you pack your own case twenty seven times. On the actual day of departure you're still not happy are you? You're panicking. 'What have I forgot, I knew I shouldn't have left all the packing this late' – eh?

Why do most women pack their cases so soon? Because they change their minds every day afterwards – that's why!

Large denomination notes

Be careful when you change your Sterling or travellers cheques into euros. The notes available in the euro currency are as follows–

5 euro note
10 euro note
20 euro note
50 euro note
100 euro note
200 euro note
500 euro note

Many shops and restaurants will not accept notes over the one hundred euro note. If you spent any serious amount of time in the Eurozone then you would hardly ever see either a two hundred euro note or a five hundred euro note. Why? Because they're all hidden underneath foreigners beds or locked away in a foreigners safe. There is so much so called 'black money' abroad that as soon as a high denomination note appears, it suddenly disappears again into the black economy. It's possibly as well really. I have seen tourists walk into a bar, buy two small beers and then offer to pay with a five hundred euro note. They cannot understand why the owner gets all arsy with them. Can you imagine walking into a pub in the UK, ordering two small beers and then offering to pay with a five hundred pound note (if there was such a thing). You'd get punched!

Make sure when you change your money into euros that you are not given any two hundred or five hundred euro notes – they're next to useless!

Last day at work

You really don't want to be there do you? The last day at work before your well earned holiday is sheer hell. You're on the beach already and you feel as though you have running shoes on so that you can leg it out of the place as soon as humanly possible. Should you suddenly develop a serious headache or pretend to drop something on your foot? Should you just play a psychological game with the boss by being grumpy to the point where he or she will let you leave early just to get rid of you? Your hearts not in it and you want to go home.

It's not as bad as the first day back though is it? More of that later!

Lemons

There are lemons growing on every street corner in many foreign towns and they are marvellous. Beware of the huge ones though! You will walk into a shop or supermarket and see loads of lemons including these particularly huge gynormous lemons. They look great, but when you cut into them the actual lemon fruit inside is tiny as most of the bulk is pith – no I haven't got a lisp! It's very disappointing as you have bought these huge enormous lemons to put into your gin and tonic or whatever and all you are getting is pith.

You don't want pith in your drink do you? I don't anyway!

Li-lo

Why don't they sell li-lo's with on board navigation units? Have you ever done it – whooo – it's dangerous! You get onto your airbed and ponce around for a while splashing and pretending that you're a red Indian in a canoe and then you just lie on it and drift for a while with your eyes closed. 'Aah, this is great'. The ripple of the water is relaxing and you just lay there dreaming and feeling smug with yourself – 'aah'. Ten minutes later, fifteen minutes later, whatever; you open your eyes and it's 'Oh hell, who stole the beach?' Panic stations, ooh, er, ooh, paddle and splash like crazy to find the land. Within two seconds you have visions of being Robinson Crusoe for the next four years until you realize that you were facing the wrong way and the beach was behind you.

Oh, that's all right then. I knew that all the time really!

Life guards

Have you seen these life guards on foreign beaches? They sit in a chair on top of a tower which has God knows how many steps going up to the top. The Mediterranean Sea in particular is usually very calm indeed and on most days it's impossible to spot even one wave. Also, there are no killer sharks in the Med' (I hope) so why on earth does he have to sit on top of a stupid tower? Let's think this through. If someone gets into trouble out in the sea and this life guard guy spots them, then it seems to me that he has two choices –

Option 1 - He can jump off his tower and break his ankle or his leg.

Option 2 - He can lift his bottom off the chair, climb down fifteen to twenty steps, leg it down the beach and then swim out to the person in trouble.

Option 1 wouldn't help his cause a great deal in the life saving stakes would it? If, on the other hand, he chose Option 2, then by the time he reached the struggling swimmer they would without doubt be drowned and completely brown bread!

So - next time you see one of these elevated life savers, just throw him up a book or a can of lager because he's about as much use as a chocolate tea pot sitting up there!

Life jackets on a boat

If you go on a fishing trip or a dolphin trip then do you look around for the life jackets as soon as you get on board the boat – I do! What is the legislation for life jackets anyway? Some of the boats I have been on whilst on holiday do not appear to have enough life jackets to go round. I count them. Four stacks of seven, that's twenty eight. I then start counting the passengers on view. 'Oh hell, I'm going to die!' On top of that, the ones which are on view don't look as if they would take the weight of a dead dog.

Take a li-lo with you just in case!

Light bulbs (foreign)

They're old fashioned, daft, and dangerous! No bayonet, push them in and twist type light bulbs over there. Oh no, these foreign type light bulbs screw in and once you have done that, they don't work. You then screw it in as far as you can with force and it connects for half a second before it crushes and you have to leg it to the nearest hospital because you have cut three fingers off your hand. You're bleeding to death. They really are stupid.

Watch yourself if yours blows!

Limping on holiday

This usually applies to women. Many, if not most women, go out and buy at least one new pair of sandals in the UK prior to going away on holiday. There's nothing wrong with that at all as you want to look your best don't you? The problem is that your feet swell when you're in the heat and you don't take that into account when you buy the sandals do you? They fit perfectly in the UK but over there they feel as though they are made from barbed wire. Result – limping! On any evening you can see British women all over foreign holiday resorts limping around as they are determined to wear their new sandals. Their feet are absolutely killing them and rather than look very nice in their new sandals they actually look like Captain Hook with a wooden leg.

Throw them back in the case until next year and then you can do it all over again, can't you ladies?

Liquid long jump

It's not a pleasant subject but sometimes holiday makers can't help it. It can be caused by underestimating the strength of cocktails, underestimating the strength of foreign beer, or just plain greed. Never mind, you're on holiday so why not get legless once or twice? The trouble is that once you feel legless there is still more alcohol in your stomach waiting to go into your system – you're wasted! Beuh, beuh, beuh – quick, leg it to the toilets. You don't get there before it comes up your throat and you have to try 'the liquid long jump'. If the toilet door is closed then it makes a hell of a mess of your clothes.

Having a great time eh?

Little twonker

Do you always get him (or her) sat behind you on the plane?

There you are, sat as comfortable as it's possible to be on a plane and the little twonker is in the seat directly behind you 'Oh no!' They never stop kicking the back of your seat and you have a headache before you've even taken off. Why don't their parents stop them doing it? If they had a little twonker sat behind them, they wouldn't like it would they? They don't say anything or do anything because it's not affecting them – that's why.

I think little twonkers should be made to sit on the wing unless they behave themselves!

Lookie lookie men

You get these African 'Lookie Lookie' men in virtually all of the popular foreign holiday resorts. They're only trying to make a living but don't they get on your damn nerves? They sell scam CD's, wood carved elephants and all kinds of things. You can be sat in a bar or café and not see a Lookie Lookie man for half an hour when one arrives selling CD's. 'No thanks, I don't want a CD'. Two minutes later and another one arrives also selling CD's, 'no thanks, I don't want a CD'. Two minutes later and another one arrives also selling CD's and your box has gone by this time – 'I don't want a ******* CD; I didn't want one from your brother, I didn't want one from his mate either, so just go away – please!' Then there are the sunglasses Lookie Lookie men. You can be laid on a sun bed with your sunglasses on and everyone else along your line of sun beds also has sunglasses on. The Lookie Lookie man walks along the whole line and asks everyone if they would like to buy some sunglasses. How many pairs of sunglasses do they think that you can wear at any one time?

Turn the tables. What you should say to them is 'Lookie ******* lookie, I've already got some!'

Looking to buy?

It's not unusual for tourists whilst on holiday to look into estate agents windows at the price of local property. You can dream can't you? Someone once said to me **'If you don't dream, you should'** – that's true! Why not take a look at the local properties available and compare prices to those in the UK? Remember this when you are looking though – it is not unusual for estate agents abroad to add <u>TEN</u> percent commission onto the selling price of a house or apartment. That's ludicrous, but it is true.

This probably sounds a bit cynical to you, but if you are actually looking to purchase a property abroad, assume that everything you are being told isn't true. If you work on that principle then you are far less likely to get ripped off. Thousands and thousands of Brits get striped when purchasing property abroad. No planning permission, building directly in front of your property once you have handed over your hard earned money, you name it and there's a con going on. If at the end of a transaction you find that everything you were told was true, then look upon that as a bonus.

Remember this statement when purchasing property abroad, *'If his lips move; he's probably lying!'*

For further information on this subject, read my first book - 'Life's a laugh on the Costa – honest!'

Loud, rough Scuzbucket family

You first spot the Scuzbuckets in the departure lounge of the airport on your way out for your well earned holiday. You think very little of it and just avoid them as they look as if they would certainly whack you one if you glanced in their general direction. You have forgotten all about them until you get to your departure gate and there they are again, well popped up and making a lot of noise. 'Oh no, they're on our plane.' You may be unlucky and get this lot sat behind you or you may be very lucky and be at the other end of the plane in which case you forget all about them again. The flight touches down and everyone makes their way to the carousel for their cases and guess what; there they are again, even more boisterous after a shed full of booze on the plane. You get out into the car park having been told which coach you're on and its – 'Oh no – the Scuzbuckets are on the same coach as us.' Panic sets in now. You really are getting quite annoyed now and praying that they get off at a hotel before or after yours. 'Surely I don't have to spend a fortnight with this bunch of idiots.'

Guess what? You do!

M

Madeira cake

For breakfast?

You go down to the restaurant at your foreign hotel on the first morning and usually find that there is a buffet style breakfast laid out for you. You may have paid a premium for four star and find that they have SSF (see SSF's later) fully cooked breakfasts. If, on the other hand, you are two or three star, then inevitably you will see sliced cheese, ham and – what, what? Madeira cake? I don't actually mind Madeira cake; I wouldn't go out of my way to have some but it's not offensive. However, for breakfast, come on! Where are my Shreddies? It ruins your morning. You have to be a bit strange don't you to wake up first thing in the morning and think to yourself, 'Yum yum, I must rush downstairs for my Madeira cake' – its not right – is it?

Maid at 9 am

Now come on! If you are on holiday then the chances are that you will want to have a little lay in on a few mornings. If you go on a bender one night then you will definitely want a lay in because the chances are that you won't have even got back to your hotel until daft o'clock. What always happens when you want to stay in bed? There's a knock on the door whilst you are in a complete coma and you just ignore it. There's another knock on the door but you ignore that as well because you're so out of it that you don't even know if it is a knock on the door or whether it's that little (I'll teach you to get drunk) man inside your head with his great big sledgehammer and a gong. It always seems to happen on the morning that you want to stay in bed. The maid wants to clean your room first! You were so ratted when you got back to your room that you didn't even think to put the 'Do not disturb' sign on your door knob. In fact you were so blathered that you probably ate it!

Some maids let themselves into your room if they don't get a response to the knocking and you can't blame them really. They have a job to do and the sooner they start, the sooner they will be able to go home to their family. I guess it's fair for them to assume that nobody is in the room if they don't get a response. I bet they see some right sights don't you? Most middle aged to older couples will not have this 'maid' problem but many younger couples do tend to go on benders whilst on holiday and I think I did it myself.

What about the groups of guys who go on holiday for a stag do? Whoooooooooooh!

It's 9.00 am in the morning and Christina is just starting work on the first floor. There she is outside the first room (yours) with her cleaning trolley and she knocks on the door or rings the bell. Nothing! She knocks on the door again or rings the bell. Nothing! In goes the skeleton key and she opens the door. She forces the beer cans and half empty take away trays into the room from behind the door and walks in gingerly. 'Mama mia!' There's bodies all over the place and none of them have any clothes on. There's one guy with a sombrero half on his head, a half eaten pizza in one hand and his willy in the other. There's another guy with lip stick on and his eyebrows shaved off because his mates thought it was really funny to do that because he passed out first, one guy sat up asleep on the toilet with his shorts around his ankles, and then two more guys stark naked on the floor with their arms around each other because they were missing their wives when they got home and couldn't see properly.

I bet Christina has a good look – I betcha!

Man boobs

Is it just me who didn't notice? It's only during the last few years that I have noticed many, if not most men, over the age of around forty five have got these man boobs. Have they always been there? It's a strange phenomenon this man boob thing. Not all of these booby type blokes are fat either. Is it something they have started to put into the water supply or do some men actually pay for a boob job these days? If so, they're being ripped off. Surely they don't pay for these sack type, baggy booby thingies do they? If they do, then it's obvious to me that cosmetic surgeons make a far better job of women than they do of men.

Marmite

Take some with you! It is possible to buy Marmite abroad but very difficult indeed as it has to be imported you know. They don't have any Marmite mines abroad. It could take you your full two weeks holiday to find a shop that sells Marmite and Marmite is great, so don't forget to pack it. If, for some unknown reason you don't like Marmite, then let me know and I"ll buy it from you.

Masons

There must be Masons abroad so I guess you're okay if you are a Mason and going abroad for a holiday. The reason I say that is because I was once having a chat with a friend on the sea front in Fuengirola where I live, said 'Goodbye', and was walking away when I was immediately stopped by a quite elderly gentleman with a Northern Ireland accent. 'You're English aren't you?' I confirmed that I was and he then said, 'I understand there is a kind of church in Fuengirola attended by gentlemen, do you know where it is?' I told him that the only English type church I knew of was in Calahonda which is about a fifteen minute drive away. 'No, this is a special type of church attended by gentlemen'. Was it my imagination, did he have some kind of affliction, was he winking and shaking his head at me, I'm not sure. Then it clicked, the penny dropped! You mean the Masons don't you? 'Yes', he said. I cracked up and couldn't resist winding him up. I said to him that as far as I was aware the Masons were a secret society and as such, by definition, the location of their hideout would be secret so how would anyone other than a Mason know where to find it. He didn't have a terrific sense of humour and looked confused. 'Tell me', I said, 'If you manage to find this hole in the wall gang, how will you manage to do all that stupid rolling your trouser leg up stuff if you're wearing shorts? Is there a special alternative sign for warm climates like waving your thingy about or something?' He was well upset at this and walked off in a huff.

Don't Masons have a sense of humour or wasn't he a proper one – how can you tell? Is it an urban myth, or do they really do all that trouser leg, silly hand shake, secret agent kiddies stuff?

Massage

On many foreign beaches you will get the Chinese massage man or lady. These people walk up and down the beach all day giving people a massage on their sun beds. That's all fine and dandy, but if you're asleep they come up to your sun bed and wake you up!

'Yu wan splecial mlassage for mlaking you fleel leraxed?'

'No I don't, I was perfectly relaxed before you came along and woke me up you wassock.' It's not on is it? There you are, asleep and as relaxed as it is possible to be when this person comes along and wakes you up in order to 'lerax' you.

I'm surprised they don't get srapped or plunched!

Medication

Lotions, potions, tablets; you name it and it's usually much cheaper abroad than it is in the UK. People are amazed how cheap certain drugs and medications are abroad. Don't ask me how that is bearing in mind that the UK has the National Health Service, but it's true. Many UK holiday makers buy pharmaceuticals in bulk and take them home. It's something which will shortly be as popular as taking cigarettes and booze back for resale to your friends.

You can get life in prison for smuggling drugs. How long can you get for smuggling hemorrhoid cream then?

Miner's helmet

Have you got one or can you borrow one?

On your foreign holiday a miner's helmet is a must accessory. You will be lucky to see out your two week holiday without there being at least one power cut. When it comes to electricity supplies, abroad is third world. The most frustrating thing is when the electricity goes off in your hotel room or apartment. You fumble around (unless you have a miner's helmet) in the dark for hours on end thinking the power cut is affecting the whole building or area and then find out that it's only your room. Yes, the trip switch in your room has tripped and you didn't realize – that's seriously annoying. That's a double use for the miner's helmet as you can now safely nut the junction box door without hurting your head!

Mini golf

Some people think that mini golf on holiday is great and other people think that it is downright stupid. Personally, I haven't really got an opinion on mini golf. If you want a game of mini golf then have a game of mini golf and to be fair, many of these holiday mini golf places have a bar in the corner and allow you to take a drink around with you. Some of them even have a little shelf type thingy at each hole for you to put your glass on and then design the course in such a way that you can go around the first half of the course and the ninth hole is back near to the bar again so that you can get a fresh pint to take with you around the last half of the course. Now I call that considerate!

I've changed my mind – I do like mini golf!

Missed a day?

Most of us have done it at some point in time whilst on holiday haven't we? Gone out one evening, had a nice meal, a few drinks, and then a few drinks more. Then – more drinks and even more drinks until its four o'clock in the morning before you know what's happened. You finally get back to your hotel room or apartment at daft o'clock and decide that it would be a good idea to have a night cap on the balcony. You then sit there talking complete and utter rubbish (often to yourself) for an hour or two and finally collapse into a coma. When you do eventually wake up, it's early the following evening and you've missed a complete day.

Where did it go – 'I can't remember; I think I got wrecked?'

Mobile telephones (for wrinklies)

You rarely see older people in the UK walking around with a mobile telephone in their hand. Why is that? It may be that many older people don't even posses a mobile telephone or it may be that they leave them at home when they go out which defeats the object somewhat doesn't it? However, it's not unusual to see older people with mobile telephones whilst on holiday in case their little grandson Jimmy is taken ill or if their neighbour needs to contact them in order to inform them of the fact that Mrs. Soandso opposite didn't put her wheelie bin out last night. Whilst on holiday you will often see older people trying to make a call or trying to receive a call on their mobile telephone and not only do they not appear to be able to understand the keyboard but they can't even see the buttons. They sit there with an incredibly screwed up face willing their eyes to focus on the keyboard and pressing the wrong buttons cutting off either themselves or the caller. By the look on their face they're in complete agony.

It's a fact that year on year mobile telephones get smaller and smaller which is all well and good for most of the population, but what about the older mobile telephone user. Come on; Motorola, Nokia, Samsung, whoever, let's have a big daft old fogy's mobile telephone with huge buttons and a screen like a TV.

Let's try and help these poor people to get connected!

Mobility scooters

Whilst on your foreign holiday you might think that it's dangerous crossing the roads because generally speaking, foreign drivers couldn't give a monkeys if they run you over or not. However, the roads are quite tame in many foreign holiday resorts compared to the pavements. Where have all the mobility scooters come from? Are there more lame people these days? If so, why?

It seems to me that about one in every five tourists I see whilst on holiday is driving a mobility scooter. There are so many of them that it's sometimes far safer to walk on the road. Most are fine and appreciate that the pavement was originally invented for pedestrians. Others however, are like demolition derby drivers and head straight for you. Who has the right of way on a pavement anyway? Is it the pedestrian or the mobility scooter driver? I don't think anybody knows. The fact is that some of these people are convinced that they have the right of way and who the hell are we to argue when we are walking along in a pair of shorts and flip flops. Many drive around in pairs, side by side, and when you see these two heading straight for you with a shopping basket on the front filled with all sorts of stuff and possibly an umbrella sticking out; you move, you move quickly. Where can I go? I have a building on my left so it's into the road I guess. You don't have the time to think about whether you would prefer to be run over by a car or a mobility scooter.

Are there hit and run mobility scooter drivers?

Can you drink and drive on a mobility scooter?

Do they have to pass a test?

I have the greatest respect for anyone with any kind of disability, but come on; how often have you been on holiday and seen someone on the terrace of a café or bar sat in a mobility scooter:

two coffees, two beers or whatever. All of a sudden this person just stands up and walks to the toilet – eh?

Who am I to judge, but you have to wonder don't you?

Monk on

Some couples just don't get on and that's a fact of life. Let's be honest though, if you don't get on whilst you're on holiday then you may as well sack it hadn't you? It's not unusual whilst on your holiday to see another couple in a bar or at the dinner table who have obviously just had a fall out. They don't speak to each other, they give each other the daggers and there's a red mist of tension hovering around them. You haven't got a clue what's gone on but it's obvious that they can't stand the sight of each other. Is it a temporary state of affairs or are they always like that? The last thing you want to do is stare at them, but you can't help it. If you are in fairly close proximity to this mutually hostile type couple then it has one of two effects on you –

1. You think it is highly amusing and you can't stop looking at them. You try not to stare but you can't help it in case you miss something which will make you smile and titter to yourself.

2. Because they are hostile and in a bad mood it puts you in a bad mood as well. It's true isn't it? If you see someone who is obviously in a bad mood then it puts you in a bad mood as well.

Why don't you move? You don't have to sit there staring at them you know.

Monkey

Has a monkey been in my bath?

If you're on holiday and running a little late prior to going out for the evening, then it's not unheard of for the man to say to the lady 'could you leave the water in the bath please and I'll just jump in for a minute after you'. Why doesn't she tell you that she has shaved her legs? 'Aaaaarrrrrrrrgh, hell, aaaaarrrrrrh!' Sometimes you don't notice all the hairs whilst you are actually in the bath, but once you stand up and look down you are covered in these little hairs and can't understand where they have all come from.

Do women do it just for a laugh? Why don't they tell you? You wouldn't get in would you?

Mosquitoes

The dirty, horrible, sneaky, blood sucking little devils!

I absolutely loath and detest mosquitoes (nearly as much as the weirdo in pink bull fighter). How do they get away with it anyway? The mosquito lands on your skin even if you're awake and you can't feel it. It then draws back its head and **wham** – it drills into your skin and sucks blood out of you – yuk! I read somewhere that mosquitoes only make that buzzing noise when they are full – full of your blood that is! Apparently when they are full, they have difficulty flying because they are so heavy and the buzzing noise is caused by that fact. Now think about this because it really isn't fair. This dirty little parasite drills a hole into you when you're asleep and sucks blood from your body. Once he has had his fill, he then has the nerve to buzz around your face and wakes you up.

I call that taking the ****!

Mosquito bites

Talking about taking the ****.

You can buy absolutely loads of different lotions and potions for putting on mosquito bites but then whilst on holiday, someone once suggested to me that putting your own urine on the bite was one of the best cures possible. This person was absolutely adamant that wee wee is an excellent antiseptic but I daren't try it. However, once I got home, I went on the internet and sure enough this person was right. Can you believe that? According to certain web sites, urine is a very good alkaline antiseptic which has been used for hundreds of years by certain people including the Eskimos. Apparently, there is even a guy in Melbourne, Australia who calls himself a 'Urine therapist'. This guy claims to drink a glass of his own urine every day and has done so for years. There are even people who consider themselves to be 'Urinophiles'. Don't start doing this just so that you can put one of these fancy titles on your CV because it certainly wouldn't impress me!

Anyway, there you go. If you do get bitten by a mosquito on your holiday, then just rub a little bit of urine onto it. Don't pass the tip on though, because if everyone starts doing it, every holiday resort in the whole world will stink like a toilet.

N

Naked lock out

Some people sleep walk and some people get absolutely and completely off their trolleys prior to returning to their hotel room whilst on holiday. The result can be suddenly finding yourself in the corridor in the early hours of the morning with the door locked behind you. You're confused. 'One minute I was asleep and now I'm out here – how?' You then look down and realize that you're stark naked. 'Aaaaaaaargh – Oh hell – erm – aaaaaaargh.' What to do? If you are very lucky and your partner is not in a coma then you will be back inside before anyone sees you. If, however, your partner is in a coma, then you have one serious problem indeed. Do you keep ringing the door bell and bashing the door down, do you hide in a broom cupboard, or do you go down to reception with your hands covering your naughty bits as best you can?

This is seriously embarrassing but lots and lots of people have done it – have you?

Name cards

Once you have collected your suitcases from the conveyor belt at the destination airport, you walk through to the arrivals lounge pushing your trolley. As soon as you go through the doors there are all kinds of people there waiting for someone or other? There are also people stood there with a flash card in front of them with someone's name on it. You look for your name don't you? You're on a package holiday and know for a cast iron fact that nobody is waiting for you apart from the tour rep who is also waiting for two hundred other tourists. Why do we waste our time scanning all the flash cards looking for our name? It's not there; it can't be. Even if it is, then it's someone else with the same name as you. Stop looking, it's pointless!

I would like to stand there with a flash card saying 'Nosey Parker' or 'What are you looking at' written on it.

Name straps (on suitcases)

Where do people get these things from and why do they buy them? You must have seen them. They're usually red or blue with the name of the suit case owner printed/embroidered along the length of the strap which is wrapped around their case. I don't know how much they cost, but obviously they must cost something and yet in most cases they are wrapped around the shabbiest suitcases on the airport conveyor belt. Why don't they just buy a new suitcase instead? I would be ashamed to put my name on some of these suitcases. If that was mine, the last thing I would want is for everyone to know that it belonged to me. These people appear to be proud of their shabby suitcases and actually want everyone to know that it belongs to them. The only logical reason I can think of is that some tour operators must run a 'Who's got the worst suitcase competition', but I've never been invited to take part!

Nappies

Why is it that some young mothers put dirty babies nappies in the litter bins on beaches? It can be right next to your (my) sun bed but they still do it. I think it is dirty, inconsiderate and damn right unhygienic.

The litter bins on beaches are for my empty beer cans aren't they?

New arrivals

People who live abroad say that they can always tell the new arrivals because they are pure white. That's simplistic and only partly true. New trainers, loads of them! You can see a British family walking along any foreign sea front and there they are; brilliant white, brand new trainers. They look like an advert for Addidas, Reebok or Nike. All walking in a line and occasionally looking down at their feet to admire their new white trainers.

Just arrived eh?

Newcastle United shirts

I will talk about foreign pedestrian crossings in more detail later but Newcastle United fans; be very careful! There should be a government health warning on Newcastle United shirts. I keep meaning to look at some road statistics on pedestrian crossing deaths. I'm sure there must be far more Newcastle United fans killed or injured on pedestrian crossings whilst on holiday than anyone else. Think about it! If you stand or walk across a pedestrian crossing in a black and white horizontally striped shirt then to any car coming towards you; you don't exist. I guess Newcastle United fans can't win really. If they try to cross the road on a pedestrian crossing in their black and white striped shirt they suddenly become invisible and they get run over because nobody can see them. If they play safe and avoid the pedestrian crossings, they get run over anyway.

To all Newcastle United football fans - Wear a Holland or a Blackpool football shirt on holiday – they're orange!

Next resort

Don't go there or you will be seriously hacked off!

It's a fact. If you are on holiday and decide to visit the next resort in order to take a skeg, then it can put you in an atrocious mood. When you get there it could be nicer than the one that you're staying in. If you visit the next resort towards the end of your holiday then it's not too bad because you have learnt something and may wish to go there next time. However, if you visit it at the beginning of your holiday then that's it – you're sulking. What do you do? You can either sulk for the next ten days or spend half of your holiday spending money commuting in a taxi every day. If you do commute, then you will find yourself being nasty to everyone else in the resort because they are staying somewhere better than you.

You paid your money and you took your choice; it was a rubbish choice – live with it!

Newspapers (British)

What on earth possesses you to buy a British newspaper whilst you're abroad on your well earned holiday? You came on holiday to get away from work and all the rubbish going on around you in the UK. It depresses you and makes you annoyed reading a newspaper when you're at home so why the hell do you punish yourself by reading one whilst on holiday? It's not logical is it? Besides that, abroad you are paying a fortune for your British newspaper. In other words you are paying a lot more money for the privilege of being depressed at a time when you actually want to relax and be happy. Why?

Buy a copy of VIZ, at least that's a laugh!

Newspaper (on the beach)

I think it would be fair to say that we are all capable of reading a newspaper without too much trouble. The problem is that we are all used to reading our newspaper indoors and when we get to our holiday destination we invariably read it on the beach. So what's the difference? Wind! There are few things more amusing on holiday than watching someone trying to read their newspaper on the beach when there's a breeze. Open the paper – woooow – grapple, grapple, bend, flop, inside out, upside down and then it's off flying all over the place. He (or she) then tries to scrunch what's left of it back together again but it looks more like a broken kite or a cauliflower than a newspaper. You've just paid a fortune for it and now it's knacked!

Newspaper (on the plane)

On some holiday flights they supply you with a newspaper once you're sat on the plane. That's very kind of them and an extremely nice gesture. But! Why is it that whichever newspaper I buy in the airport terminal, it's the same one they give me once I get on the plane? I'm beginning to get a complex about it. Does someone follow me around the terminal building in order to see which newspaper I buy then make sure they give me exactly the same one once I board. I've tried the Daily Mail, the Daily Express, and even the Times, but whichever one I choose they give me the same one. Why and how is that?

Does that happen to you? Oh, you buy a comic – that's okay then!

'No, you can't go in the swimming pool because it's raining!'

Have you ever said that to your children or heard someone else saying it to their children? What's it all about; it's not logical: is it? Let's just say it again slowly and then we can all think this one through -

'NO, YOU CAN'T GO IN THE SWIMMING POOL BECAUSE IT'S RAINING!'

You are fairly unlucky if it rains on your holiday in a hot climate, but if it does, then why can't your children play in the swimming pool? Water is wet, and water is water, whether it's falling out of the sky as rain or just sat there minding its own business in a swimming pool. If your child goes into the swimming pool then I think it would be safe to say that they will get wet, so what's the difference?

Why can't you go into the swimming pool when it's raining? It's not fair, and it certainly isn't logical.

O

'Offside'

Whatever you do guys, if you go on holiday during either the European Championships or the World Cup, don't take your wife into a bar to watch the match. If you do then you had better hope and pray that there isn't a controversial offside decision. The whole bar will jump up and down shouting 'offside' or 'that was never offside'. At that moment in time I can absolutely guarantee that your wife will turn round to you and say 'what's offside?' That is definitely your football match well and truly shafted. Have you ever tried explaining the offside rules to a woman? You may as well try to discuss Einstein's theory of relativity or the merits of going on a golfing holiday with your mates.

Watch the match on your own – it's far less complicated!

Out of your depth

Ooooooh, what's down there? We all do it – I think? We walk into the sea gingerly feeling our way out for a swim. We don't like the feel of some of the things under foot because we think there could be some nasty armoured crawly things or a jelly thingy or some slimy seaweed. Then you get to the point where you have to let go of the floor with your feet and swim because the water is too deep. Ooooooh, which is worse? Is it feeling the slimy knobbly things under foot or the thought of something else underneath you whilst you're swimming.

Shark fins, jelly fish, toilet paper – ooooh it's scary!

Overhead lockers

Some people get irate about overhead lockers on the plane. 'That's my bit; the cheeky sod has put his hand luggage into my bit!' So what, does it matter? There can be oodles of space in the next locker or the one across the aisle, but that guy has put his stuff into your bit, above your head, it's not fair. I know – it's because when the plane lands you want to be straight up into the locker above your head for your bag, then first off the plane. You can't get off the plane until they open the door and you're not supposed to stand up until the door is open anyway.

You're a bit sad you know!

P

Palm trees

There are millions of them abroad. They're those big trees with long straight trunks, long flowing leaves and you can't grow them in Halifax. Well, I couldn't anyway!

Paragliding

Have you ever done that? I love paragliding but there is one strange phenomenon that is not unique to me because I have seen lots of other people doing it. Once you have finished your standard issue ten minutes or whatever, the speedboat guy brings you back towards the shore. You've had a great time and you feel exhilarated – but - once he gets fairly near to the shore he slows down and you start to descend. What do you do? I bet you do the same as me and start looking around for shark fins hovering in the sea beneath you. I've had a great time but I am now pooing my pants in case I see a sharks fin in the water.

Is that normal?

Pass the parcel (I mean baby)

Ladies, when you're on a plane please don't start telling the parents of babies that you think the baby is beautiful. It's not fair on us men. There we are on the plane with our first beer or gin and tonic when all of a sudden, following your wife going 'Goo

goo' or 'Round and round the garden like a teddy bear', a baby is being passed half way around the plane over people's heads – usually mine. I'm going on holiday and trying to enjoy a drink for God's sake!

Baby pass the parcel – we men don't like it. We're on holiday as well you know!

Passport control men (foreign)

You hate them don't you? They're such surly, miserable wassocks. We all promise ourselves to get him back this time and not smile at him. Then, at the last minute, you do smile at him and he gives you another one of those plonker looks. He got you again didn't he?

Don't smile at him – coward! He can't stop you entering or leaving his country just because you don't smile at him.

Pedalos

Pedalos are great. What more could you want than to just cruise and float around in the sun with not a care in the world. Pedal for a while, float for a while, dive in and swim around for a while, and all for a few euros or whatever. You can get blue pedalos, yellow pedalos, red pedalos and every colour pedalo you could ever wish for. Then there are the different shaped ones; pedalos with a water slide on the back, big stupid ones which look like a tractor, other big daft ones which look like a Noddy car; you name it and you can get a pedalo which looks similar. Pedalo design has come a long way over the last ten years or so but one thing never changes – if your foot slips off one of those pedals, it gets trapped between the pedal and the boat and it makes you swear a lot (see also jelly fish). 'Ouch, ****, I think I've broken my ankle?' There is an upside to slipping your foot off the pedal though. If, after pedaling for half an hour or so you make a big issue out of **pretending** to slip off the pedal and hurting your ankle, then you can draw the sympathy card and get your wife to pedal back. If you make a really, really, really big issue out of pretending to hurt your ankle, then when you get back to the shore you can play the huge sympathy card and be allowed to go for a nice pint or twelve. Good eh?

Pedalos – they make you swear a lot and can earn you a few sympathy pints - I mean points!

Pedestrian crossings

Foreign pedestrian crossings – don't believe them – they don't mean it!

It's bad enough in the UK these days crossing the road, but go abroad if you want some real frights. They're complete lunatics! To be fair, you know where you stand with most foreign drivers as they are quite open and honest about the fact that they will run you over on a pedestrian crossing without feeling any guilt whatsoever. But then there are the real bad natured foreigners who lull you into a false sense of security by slowing down a bit whilst approaching the crossing. They're having a laugh – they don't mean it really. The chances are that he's only slowing down because he's scratching his bottom or picking a cigarette off the floor of his car because he dropped it. He has no intention of stopping for a tourist like you, or anyone else for that matter. I don't want to believe that they do it on purpose, I don't think they do. They're just oblivious to anything that is happening outside of their own little world – their car. You can look him in the eye, stand there on the crossing waving your arms around or you could even get your willy out if you wanted to, but you're still dead meat to him.

He isn't going to stop, so you best leg it – quickly!

People who earwig and then join in your conversation

I can't stand them. Nosey interfering nerds they are!

You can be sitting in the hotel reception, a bar or a restaurant and talking amongst yourselves when suddenly a couple on the next table will just butt into your conversation. You can be talking about a previous holiday and they will say something like, 'Oh we've been there twice, 1992 and 1993 it was, and we stayed at the Hotel Angela. It's very nice there isn't it?' Well yes it is, but who's talking to you shark face? On the other hand, you can be talking about an ailment you have had in the past, like a bad back or something. 'Oh, I've had that, but twice as bad as you'. Well you would have wouldn't you? Even family conversations aren't sacred to these people. You could be talking about your children or grand children when they pipe up, 'Oh we have eleventeen children and fifty seven grand children you know'.

Who gives a monkey's – keep your nose out – shark face!

Picasso

Pablo Picasso is Malaga's favourite son, and one of the whole of Spain's favourite sons. He is one of the most famous artists in the history of the world and the Spaniards are very very proud of him.

Am I missing something?

I want to like modern art, but I can look at a Picasso painting, stand back, look again whilst stroking my chin and think to myself, 'That's rubbish!' It is isn't it? How can it be clever to paint a lady who looks as though she has been bashed in the face with a sledge hammer and has three eyes? Call me a philistine if you want, I probably am when it comes to modern art, but however hard I try, it still looks rubbish to me!

Pierced nipples

I guess some men must find pierced nipples attractive, but I'm afraid that I'm not one of them. What possible motivation can there be for a lady to go and see a complete stranger, lop one out, and ask him to fire a piece of metal through her nipple. On every beach abroad you will see the pierced nipple lady (or man). I am absolutely frightened to death of hypodermic needles and therefore probably biased due to the nature of the things. If I went on a bachelor night out and the guys said to some woman in the pub who happened to be on a hen night, 'Get 'em out for the lads' and she did; if she had a pierced nipple I would have to ask her to put her jollies away again – yuk!

The trouble is, if you're on a beach abroad you can't get away from them, can you?

Pig pen

Have you ever been asleep or dozing off on your sun bed around the pool or on the beach when all of a sudden you're disturbed by a snort, grunt and a 'plaaaaagh'. 'What the hell is that?' You open your eyes and look around you and there he or she is – pig pen! A huge lump of lard on the next sun bed to you snoring, grunting with their mouth open, and generally looking like a bowl full of trifle and custard. Sometimes, if you're really unlucky, there may be more than one of them and it's like trying to relax in a farm yard.

Pillows (foreign)

If I don't have a decent pillow then I can't sleep properly. Can you? I have to put my arm under a naff pillow and then I wake up thinking that my arm has been amputated because it's gone all numb. Am I unusual? I like a thick pillow which doesn't go out of shape and looks like a sack of spuds after thirty seconds of having my head on it. Foreign pillows are absolute rubbish. Sometimes if you have a double bed then you get one big long pillow for the both of you. That's no good is it? You finish up having a tug of war at three o'clock in the morning and then grunting and nudging each other. It's not practical to bring your own, but be prepared for the foreign pillow because they really are heaps of junk!

Pilots

Why do I always get the same pilot?

He comes over the intercom system and it's him again. The same pilot as last time and the time before that as well. I'm sure it's him; he's got the same voice anyway. The poor man; he deserves a holiday as well. He puts a hell of a lot of hours in doesn't he? I think it's dangerous!

Or is it just that they all sound the same? If so, why?

Pi**ed (again)

On the odd occasion that I have had a few too many drinks on holiday but I think I feel okay, everyone else looks ****** to me. I'm okay, I think? Apparently, according to my wife Chris, I was once sat on a bar stool with a stupid grin on my face when someone accidentally nudged me. Allegedly I turned to this person and said 'You're ******!' This guy then turned round to me and said 'Excuse me, but I am not ******'. 'Oh', I said, 'I thought you were because your face is blurred!'

You think you're okay; it's everyone else who looks ******!

Pistols (water)

What ever happened to water pistols? When I was younger, many boys had a water pistol and they were fairly harmless because they had limited fire power and you couldn't hit a barn door from two feet away. Not any more. Technology has moved on in water firearm annoyance and most kids now have these huge blunderbuss type things. Parents always seem to buy one of these things for their children on holiday and then tell them to go and play somewhere else. The problem is that they usually come and play near me and I get seriously annoyed. You have to make allowances and let children enjoy themselves but when they have a blunderbuss and they're annoying everyone except their own parents then that's not on – is it? Chris and I once had a situation with one of these blunderbuss children on a foreign holiday and rather than chastise the child I told him to go over to his parents and tell them that if they didn't take his gun away, then I would come over and shove it up his dad's bottom – side ways! I would have done as well. What are these parents on? Their attitude appears to be, 'I don't mind you being annoying son, as long as it's not near me'.

It's just not right – is it?

Planes pulling advertising banners

It's actually a clever advertising idea, but it's also extremely infuriating on your foreign holiday. There you are nodding off on your sun bed and life couldn't be better could it? What happens when you're just about to go into the land of nod? The Mediterranean version of the Red Baron (El Red Barono) comes over just above head height in his bi-plane pulling some advertising banner in which most people have no interest whatsoever. Us Brits should bring our own First World War pilot and plane across to shoot this nauseating Red Baron guy out of the sky. You look up with a dozy expression, tut, go half back to sleep and then here he comes again having done a loop the loop u-turn.

Whatever he's advertising I wouldn't buy it, even if I was desperate for it!

Plastic carrier bags

Haven't the foreigners ever heard of protecting the environment? Plastic carrier bags, zillions of them! They're blowing around in the streets, along the beaches, hanging off lamp posts and trailing along underneath cars. You get a plastic carrier bag (or ten) with just about everything you buy abroad. It isn't necessary, but you get one anyway. I swear to God that I once went into a shop in Turkey and bought a box of matches. They gave me the matches in a plastic carrier bag.

However would I have managed without it?

Plastic shower curtains

They're a pet hate of mine, plastic shower curtains. I absolutely hate the damn things and I think they hate me too. I get into the shower after a hot day on the beach and really look forward to it.

I start running the water, get the temperature just right and then climb in. Thirty seconds tops – it attacks me and I haven't done anything wrong to it. It's like wrestling an octopus. I try turning around or anything to get away from it but it won't leave me alone. I punch it, kick it and call it a ******* but this thing has real staying power. I even threaten to throw it over the balcony but it takes no notice. The worst thing is the thought that it has probably been stuck to about two thousand other tourists before it attacked me – yuk yuk yuk!

Plastic squeezy bottles

They're absolute rubbish abroad!

Local mayonnaise, tomato ketchup, or anything that comes in a plastic squeezy bottle – uurrrrgh! They squeeze alright, but they don't expand back out to the original shape. After two or three squeezes you finish up with something which resembles a screwed up handkerchief or Nora Batty's stockings.

What's wrong with foreign plastic bottle manufacturers? They're useless!

Playing cards

Take a pack of playing cards on your foreign holiday and carry them around with you during the evenings. Especially in Spain! A good way to earn a quick euro or two is to teach a Spaniard how to play Snap. You will always win! It's a fact of life that Spaniards are completely incapable of saying the word 'snap'. It is not anywhere near their vocabulary capabilities and they have to say 'e-snap'. That's it; you've got a second start on them every time and as such, you win every time. Good eh?

I suppose if you played snap with a Spaniard who had a stammer then that would be even better '– e-e-e-e-e-e-snap!'

That's not funny is it?

Plug holes

If there is one thing in the whole world that makes me instantly feel physically sick it's human hair in the plug hole – buoooooooogh! Is it just me? I really really hate that and just the thought of it makes me shudder. If the hotel cleaner hasn't cleaned the plug holes properly prior to my arrival then I'm in big trouble because I won't even go near them. Human hair in plug holes actually put me off my favourite breakfast cereal for life. Up until my late teens I was a compulsive Shredded Wheat eater until one day when a friend said to me 'it reminds me of hair in the plug hole'. Whaaaat – aaaaargh!

I haven't touched Shredded Wheat since that day. It's not really made of human hair is it?

PMT

Oooooooh, scary scary! (see also HRT tablets)

I don't even try to analyse PMT and I don't think anyone else should either. If you're on holiday, the last thing you want is for your wife or partner to have a bout of 'Everyone's a tosser apart from me' syndrome. There isn't an answer to it, and women don't appear to know a great deal about it themselves. Some women even appear to go into denial about it. For instance: Chris used to run the accounts office at a road haulage firm in the UK prior to us moving to Spain and she had a number of women working for her. She would occasionally come home from work in one hell of a mood and come out with something like 'Aaaaaargh, PMT, those women have driven me mad today. It must be "that" time as they were all in a foul mood'. The thing is; it wasn't the other women at all, it was her. It appears to me that women don't think they suffer from PMT; it's all the other women instead!

Sometimes it's easy to detect, and can come in the simple form of something like me saying 'It's a beautiful day again; shall we just nip into a beach bar for a coffee?' She doesn't answer; all she does is shake her head and then look in the other direction. Have I suddenly turned invisible and has she suddenly gone deaf? That's it; keep your mouth shut!

Then – oh then – we have the other extreme. She was perfectly okay yesterday. We had a lovely day on the beach and then went to a very nice fish restaurant for our evening meal. You half wake up the following morning and something's different as soon as you open your eyes. There are atmospherics in the hotel room, there's a hissing noise and a sort of pale crimson mist in the air. You turn over and there she is; already sat up in bed, with her arms tightly folded across her chest – 'hiss' – you look around the room for the broom propped up in the corner and you know instinctively that today – you're a tosser!

I sometimes think that women don't really suffer from this thing called PMT at all. They just use it as an excuse to be nasty to everyone. What do you think?

You're probably only on holiday for a week or a fortnight and the last thing you want is a few days of grief. We still laugh about it now, but I can remember years ago on holiday and Chris just turned round to me out of the blue and said -

'Why did you do that?'

'Do what', I said.

'Nudge me; you just nudged me'.

'No I didn't'.

'Yes you did'.

Oh – the penny dropped. PMT!

'Er, okay I'm sorry'.

'What for?'

'For nudging you'.

'But you said that you hadn't nudged me'.

'I didn't think that I had'.

'Then why are you apologizing'.

'Because you said that I did nudge you'.

'Then you must have known that you nudged me, otherwise you wouldn't apologize'.

Oh Christ, Shut up and withdraw gracefully Stuart.

The worst was yet to come. About ten minutes later, I did nudge Chris by mistake, and that's probably the worst thing that could have happened in the whole wide world –

'Sorry' I said.

'What for?'

'For nudging you'.

'You didn't nudge me'.

'Yes, I just knocked your arm by mistake'.

'No you didn't'.

Er, oh hell, where do I go from here? I can't win - can I?

PMT on holiday. It's frightening!

Politically correct brigade

Ah – we've got you now haven't we - you man hating left handed vegetarian (if it's a woman). When you go on holiday you lot keep your thoughts to yourself don't you, because outside of the UK people can say whatever they want without being branded a racist or a fascist. Free speech exists abroad for tourists to say whatever they want to each other. You can listen to British tourists who are on holiday and if someone raises the subject of the NHS, immigration, hanging or single mothers, they go on one. Wow: someone saying what they think. What a novelty!

You politically correct merchants keep your mouths shut on a foreign holiday don't you? You know for a cast iron fact that you would get eaten alive by normal folk who for two weeks are not afraid of being branded a fox killer. Your vegetarian, bicycle clip ideals mean nothing to most real people and once offshore, you're shafted. Go on, I dare you. Sit in a tourist bar abroad and raise one of your PC subjects. You would get verbally assassinated and you know it.

Phew – I feel better for that!

Poor man in a rich man's shirt

At most foreign markets you will see stalls selling designer shirts and polo shirts for a fraction of the price you would pay for the real thing. La Coste, Thomas Burberry, Ralph Lauren, you name it. They are excellent. They not only look exactly like the real thing but they wash great as well.

It's naughty to sell them so I suppose it's also naughty to buy them, but they really are good.

Pop, pop pop!

Millions and millions of people throughout the world chew chewing gum and there is nothing at all wrong with that. However, for some strange reason which I will never understand, fully grown foreigners are obsessed with blowing bubbles with theirs and popping the damn stuff. Everywhere you go you will see the locals blowing bubbles out of their mouths and it sometimes sounds like you're surrounded by pop guns.

Why can't they suck a lolly instead?

Post cards

Have you seen them? Ooh – foreign post cards!

You can buy normal post cards which are views of your resort, but you can also get a full biology lesson on cardboard. Wow, is it legal? Some of these post cards look like a crash course in surgery and there they are in full view of everybody. Sometimes you have to pick them up and turn them around as you can't tell which way up they're supposed to be.

They're seriously naughty!

Post card to a neighbour

Send one of those filthy semi pornographic post cards to the neighbour you don't speak to (see also Dire Straits). The post man will think they're some kind of perverts and news soon spreads. You could also put something nice and traditional on the card like 'Weather is here, wish you were fine!'

Public address systems (in the airport)

Surely technology has moved on quicker than the standard of public address systems in airports hasn't it? You can be sat there in the departure lounge at virtually any UK airport all excited because you are flying out for your holiday and not have a clue what's going on. For some strange reason there appears to be two distinct audio quality levels on the public address system and I can't understand why. Useless information is perfectly audible such as 'Smoking is not allowed anywhere in this airport' or 'Please do not leave your baggage unattended' – crystal clear, no problem. Then we have the important information about flight departures, gate numbers etc. and you haven't a clue what they're talking about. It sounds like Elmer Fudd is making the announcement and everyone starts leaning to one side as if they may be able to make it out better if their ear is nearer to the loudspeaker.

Why is that?

Public toilets

They haven't been invented yet in foreign holiday resorts. Foreigners want the tourists, but for some reason they don't want them to go to the toilet. What do you do, where do you go? Tourists usually find themselves going into a bar in order to go to the toilet. The problem is that once you've been to the toilet, drank a beer and walked a hundred yards down the road, you need to go to the toilet again. So, it's into another bar for the toilet and another beer.

You get drunk doing that you know!

I reckon foreigners don't supply public toilets on purpose so that tourists will drink more of their lager. What do you think?

Q

Queue splits

Has it happened to you? You arrive at the airport reasonably early and when you get to the check in area there is only one desk open for your flight. Not too bad though, about twenty people in front of you so you'll get checked in fairly quickly. Until! It's not right; a huge queue has built up behind you and you feel quite smug. What do they do? They open another desk and all the people behind you rush to the front of the new queue.

That's not fair is it?

R

Rainbows

It doesn't rain very often in foreign holiday resorts, but when it does and a rainbow appears, it looks absolutely stunningly beautiful against the bright blue sky. Tourists look at the bright colours of the rainbow in absolute awe and of course think of the pirate treasure at the end of it. There is always a pirate treasure chest at the end of every rainbow because my Dad told me lots of times when I was young.

Now then, whilst on the subject, we were once in the beer garden at Fuengirola mini golf with some friends of ours Nikki and Lyndon. We had just had a few spots of rain and a beautiful rainbow appeared which prompted the predictable comments about the beautiful colours and pirate treasure. All of a sudden Lyndon pipes up 'You don't find treasure at the end of rainbows, you find a big set of weighing scales'. I then looked around at the others sat at the table and they in turn looked at me. 'Er – okay Lyndon – why would you find a set of weighing scales at the end of a rainbow?' His answer was very simple 'Well – when I was younger my granddad used to sing me that song –

'Somewhere, over the rainbow - weigh a pie.'

'And that's why my grandad said there was a set of weighing scales at the end of every rainbow – so that you can weigh the pie.'

Oh, that's okay then Lyndon. Good stuff this Spanish lager!

Razors

Please bring your own razor on holiday ladies!

This is one thing that really, really, really naffs me off. I have been on holiday for about two days when I have a shave one morning and look as if I have signed up for do-it-yourself surgery classes as my face is cut to ribbons. I speak to Chris and she puts that completely innocent look on her face, 'I haven't touched your razor – honest!'

My razor has mysteriously gone completely blunt. It must be the sea air?

Red eye flights

They're a killer aren't they? You have to vacate your room or apartment at midday but you are not flying back to the UK until daft o'clock. You feel like a refugee and if the weather is hot the only option you have of a shower is a communal room which is also being used by every man and his brother. It's disgusting! What do you do? Some people (but not me) get legless because there's nothing else to do and they wish that they had booked a different holiday with a more sociable flight time. The problem is that if you 'go on one' for that final afternoon and evening, then you feel like death by the time you board the plane. Once you do board the plane, half of the passengers have red eyes and are in a foul mood.

I wonder why?

Resolve

As with Germolene – take some with you!

Inevitably during your foreign holiday you will get legless on at least eleventeen occasions. Resolve is a 'must' accessory for the morning after and I have never seen it for sale abroad. You can even make a profit out of it; it's like smuggling cigarettes in reverse. Believe me, if a fellow Brit has a stonking hangover one morning then he will pay you an absolute fortune for one of your Resolve sachets.

It's a good earner!

Rivets (aircraft)

Do you do this? I do!

If you have a day time flight and get a seat on the aircraft which is over the wing, do you slowly move your eyes around all of the rivets on the wing? I don't really know what I am expecting to see and even if I did see a loose or missing rivet, would I stand up shouting something like 'Loose rivet, loose rivet – over here!' What would the other passengers think? I'll tell you exactly what they would think, 'Loose screw more like – what a nutter!'

I can sometimes take this strange habit one step further and look over to see who is sat opposite in the same row window seat as me. Are they checking the rivets as well; I hope so. Look out for loose rivets, you could save everyone's life and be a hero.

Then again you could just be paranoid – like me!

Rock

I obviously haven't visited every single tourist resort in the world so I may be wrong, but why can't you buy a stick of rock abroad?

Whenever most people go to the seaside in the UK, they buy at least one stick of rock to either eat immediately or take home. This rock usually has the name of the resort running through the middle of it but I don't think that you can buy Fuengirola rock or Skiathos rock. Then there are those big stupid sugar dummies. Why don't foreigners make big stupid sugar bulls or big stupid sugar Fez's, or big stupid sugar pyramids?

We Brits love our rock and someone could make a fortune. Couldn't they?

Roller bladers

I wish I could do that don't you? You see lots of them whilst on holiday abroad, gliding along the promenade and I get dead envious. You are now probably thinking to yourself 'If he's so envious, then why doesn't he buy a pair of roller blades himself and learn how to do it?' The answer to that question is quite simple – I know for a cast iron fact that I would break my neck and no doubt kill shed loads of tourists in the process. I'm a realist and know that roller booting is definitely not for me! That said, I can stand there completely mesmerized by these roller blade type people as it looks so easy and I guess it's also great exercise. Roller booting is a fantastic way of getting around and the really good ones just seem to hover on a cushion of air. The trouble is, if you just happen to be sauntering along on the pavement and the roller blader comes up from behind you going in the same direction, then they scare the living daylights of you. They are completely silent and you don't hear them coming until they whiz past you at thirty miles per hour and you drop your ice cream cornet in fright. 'What the hell!'

Roller bladers – they look great but pooh, are they dangerous or what?

Roof exits

I have often been in a foreign building on the top floor and seen an emergency exit leading to the roof (see also FIRE). There isn't an external fire staircase, so what's that all about? Let's just say that you're on the top floor when a fire breaks out, where do you go? Onto the roof - if so why? What are you going to do once you arrive on the roof apart from have a nervous poo in the corner once you realize there are no fire stairs?

Unless you are a bird or a human canon ball from the circus, then I would risk it down the stairs if I were you!

Roses

Whilst you are out for the evening abroad you will inevitably be approached by people offering to sell you a single red rose for your wife or partner. That's romantic isn't it? It cracks me up sometimes when I watch a couple who have obviously been together for a number of years and the man just turns round to the lady and says something along the lines of, 'Do you want one'? You have missed the point pal. The idea is not for you to ask 'Do you want one', it is for you to just buy her a nice red rose and hand it over to her saying 'Here you are darling; I love you.'

In the past I have bought Chris a red rose and I think it's nice and romantic. The problem is that when you eventually get back to your hotel room there is nowhere to put the damn thing. Not many hotel rooms just happen to have a nice empty vase sat on the table waiting for your red rose. Where do you put it? It's either in the sink or in the bidet I guess.

What a waste of money that was!

Rude T-shirts

You sometimes see people (usually men) walking around the UK in a rude-ish T-shirt. It's a bit naughty but not too offensive. However, on holiday abroad you see T-shirts which are absolutely beyond belief. It's a double take, a complete gob dropper. I am far from a prude; in fact I'm about as far away from being a prude as it's possible to get, but how on earth do the shops get away with it? It can't just be because the wording on the T-shirts is in English and the local police can't understand it, because the wording is usually accompanied by a picture of a huge willy, a bottom, or a massive pair of ladies jollies. Selling them is one thing, but who in their right mind is going to buy one and wear it? People do though; and it's not just teenagers. You can see older people walking along a foreign promenade in one of these naughty T-shirts sporting a huge grin on their face because they think it's belly laugh funny to have a picture of some cartoon type fat midget bloke with a ten foot willy across the front of his T-shirt.

Only recently I saw an old guy walking down the beach in Fuengirola with a black T-shirt on. This gentleman was at least sixty years old, had a huge beer belly and a bald head. On the back of his T- shirt it said –

Work and play -

During the day I bang nails

During the night I bang beaver

Yeah, of course you do mate!

It's not just obscene T-shirts either. You will often see people on holiday wearing a T-shirt saying something which completely contradicts the way that person looks. For instance; another guy I saw fairly recently was at least eighteen stone and he was wearing this T-shirt with 'Leeds Triathlon' across the front and back of it in large lettering. Now come on! This guy was a big guy and when I say big, I mean humungously fat. Who does he think he's kidding? Unless this Triathlon consisted of darts, snooker and wellie wanging then I think we can safely assume that he has a rather vivid imagination.

Running for a bus – in flip flops!

Hee hee! It's bad enough trying to walk in flip flops (see also flip flops), but if you're going out for the day whilst on holiday and there is just the very remotest chance that you may want to catch a bus; you're in big trouble!

'Quick, the bus is coming.' Flip, flop, flip, flop, fliiiiiip – flooooooopp - fliiiiiipetty, -floooooooppetty – skid – trip – 'Oooooooh – ouch – ******* – quick; call an ambulance.'

Rusty clothes driers

If you wash one of your best designer shirts out whilst on holiday, be careful! Check the clothes drier on your balcony if there is one. Most of the clothes driers abroad are metal mesh which is coated with plastic. During the summer months the plastic cracks with the intense heat, exposing the metal underneath and this in turn goes rusty during the winter. I have ruined countless items of clothing on these heaps of rubbish.

S

Sand in your face

There are few things better than lying on a sun bed on the beach and reading an excellent book. You may occasionally put the book down and go for a swim or possibly go for a stroll to the beach bar. What happens at the end of your extremely enjoyable day? You put the book into your beach bag and go back to your apartment or hotel room. You then take a shower and get changed prior to going out for a nice evening, probably including a meal and a few drinks. Then it's back to your apartment or hotel again and into bed for a quick read before you go to sleep ready for another perfect day tomorrow. There you are, lying in bed feeling all smug when you decide to have a quick read of your book prior to turning the light off. Your day has been as near perfect as is possible to get but it's about to be completely and utterly ruined!

Sand in your face!

You are happily lying horizontally in your bed when you pick up the book and lift it above your face, then – 'Aaargh, plaaarh, what the hell!' Half of the beach has just fallen onto your face and into your nice clean bed. The book is full of sand and you're now half blind and your bed feels as though it's full of broken glass.

Whatever happened to that perfect day? 'Ah hell.'

Sandwiches on the beach

If you hire a sun bed on the beach, you don't have to sneak

153

sandwiches you know. You can see British tourists on a sun bed and watch them look around suspiciously to clock where the attendant is. If they think he isn't looking they will take a tin foil package out of their bag, peel back one corner and then take a bite of the sandwich which they have brought with them in order to save money. It's not illegal; nobody is going to kick you off the beach for eating your own sandwiches. Just remember that the sun bed man is printing money just by having your bottom on his sun bed. Sod what he thinks, even if he does also own the bar next to your sun bed. If you want to eat your own sandwiches then eat them and be damned. Why should you give him all of your business! All in all, on your two week holiday, you could have bought two sun beds for the money you have given him.

Scandinavians with ski sticks

'Excuse me please, what on earth is that all about?'

Whilst on holiday, most people go for a walk along the promenade. It's great, 'Da de da de da; mm, mm, mm; oh look at this' or 'look at that.' Not the Scandinavians, oh no. They bring on holiday with them in the blazing sunshine – erm – ski sticks. Yes, ski sticks! They don't have any skis on their feet just flip flops or trainers but there they are, walking in an exaggerated manner waving these ski stick thingies backwards and forwards as if they're on snow.

Why, oh pray tell me why, would anyone even consider taking ski sticks on holiday with them?

Scooter hire

Don't do it – just don't do it!

There is no driving discipline abroad and the quality of roads is, generally speaking, er, rubbish! Save your Barry Sheen impersonation until you get home. There are pot holes, oil spillages and debris all over the place and if you drive around a corner too fast then you're spending your well earned holiday in hospital. Many people do and it's not worth it – just don't do it!

Scooters - listen!

If you are a lady carrying a shoulder bag and hear the sound of a motor scooter coming up behind you then stop and watch! There are foreign youngsters who drive around on scooters in pairs, one on the front driving and the other on the back with a Stanley knife. They will drive past you very slowly and the one on the back will cut straight through the strap of your bag and they are gone with the lot. They are absolute scumbags and sometimes cut the person as well as the shoulder strap.

Watch out for them!

Sea (Mediterranean)

Where does all the sea go? You could stand at the waters edge at a Mediterranean holiday resort for five solid weeks and not get wet above the knees. The waves keep coming in, not big ones I'll grant you, but the water never goes any further than a few inches behind you. If, on the other hand, you do the same thing at Blackpool then you drown – quickly! The sea knocks seven bells out of everything and if you stood at the waters edge there, the water would be above your head within a few hours. So – if you fancy standing safely at the waters edge with no tide for five weeks, the Med' is the place to visit.

That's a good selling point for the Mediterranean Tourist Boards. I think?

Seagulls

On the Costa del Sol you will struggle to see ten seagulls in one week. There are thousands and thousands of pigeons, but hardly any seagulls. Why is that? Have a look next time you go, it's very strange. If you go to a British holiday resort then all you can hear are seagulls squawking but that sound doesn't exist on some of the Costas. Why? I wish I knew. Is it that pigeons are hard cases and they beat up any seagulls who dare to travel to this part of the world? Is it that the seagulls here pretend to be pigeons? To be perfectly honest, I don't really know the difference between a seagull and a pigeon apart from the fact that seagulls squawk and here, there is no squawking! Is it that pigeons like the heat and seagulls don't? Is it that the pigeons that I think are pigeons are really seagulls with a different clacker which make it impossible for them to squawk? It's a mystery!

Should Spain import some seagulls from Whitby?

Sea shells

This tourist hobby absolutely fascinates me. You can visit any beach you want abroad and see numerous adult tourists walking along the waters edge picking up sea shells and putting them into a bag or a little plastic bucket. 'That's a nice one there'; 'Oh that one's chipped'. What do they do with all these shells once they have collected them? I can't see anyone taking five kilos of sea shells home with them on the plane. Even if they do, which is highly unlikely, what do they do with them all when they get home? Do they stick them onto a wine bottle and make a table lamp? If so why? They look tacky and naff anyway!

Second hand markets

As in the UK, there are numerous second hand markets abroad. Through your holiday rep you will get the opportunity to book excursions to all kinds of places including the markets which take place on different days in different towns. That's all well and good but just make sure that you ask the question 'Which market is it?' Some markets are actually second hand markets and although you may be a flea market fan back home, it is probably the last thing you want to see whilst on holiday. Remember that many foreign countries are relatively poor and the difference between the rich and the poor is far greater than it is in the UK. The result is that if you are unfortunate enough to find yourself in a foreign second hand market then you will find stalls selling wall to wall absolute and utter tat. Tractor tyres, old yokes for putting around horses or a cows neck, old prams, clothes which you wouldn't even throw on a bonfire and bags full of rusty nuts and bolts. I don't think so do you?

Ask the question because if you don't; it will seriously ruin your day!

Second time 'arounders'

Separation and divorce are very common place in the UK, but you can usually spot the 'second time arounders' whilst you're on holiday. Middle aged couples groping and slobbering each other in a bar or restaurant and acting like two teenagers. They stand out like a sore thumb as all the other couples are just sat there staring into space and not saying a word to each other apart from 'Look at those two over there; it's disgusting'. It's not disgusting at all! They have probably both gone through years of hell with someone they couldn't stand the sight of and are now enjoying their little bit of freedom and excitement. However, having said that, some of them do appear to go through some kind of second coming in the dress sense department. They have begun a new era in their lives and they suddenly feel ten years younger but what they don't realize, is that they don't actually look ten years younger. Some people appear to give custody of their common sense to someone else when they get divorced.

Then there are the young second time arounders. These tend to be in their twenties and usually have three or four children with them. Generally speaking; the days of couples having lots of children have been and gone to be replaced with young second time arounders who have a brood of mixed parentage. The ladies children tend to huddle around her whilst the fathers' children don't really know what the hell to do because they only usually see their Dad once a flood. Good on him for bringing his child/children as well, but there doesn't appear to be a lot of harmony in the new family unit -

157

Lady's child	'If I can't have another coke I'll tell my dad.'
Lady's new partner	'Your dad's in England (we think), so you can't.'
Lady's child	'If you were my proper dad you would let me have another coke.'
Lady's new partner	'Well I'm not your proper dad, so you can't.'
Lady	'Go on; let him have another coke.'
Lady's new partner	'No. If we let him have another coke, we will have to buy the other kids another coke.'
Lady	'If it was your Jimmy wanting another coke you would buy him one.'
Jimmy	'Yes you would Dad wouldn't you?'
Lady's new partner	'No I wouldn't.'
Jimmy	'My proper mum would buy me another coke.'
Lady	'Well; she would wouldn't she – fat cow.'
Jimmy and his sister	'Don't you call my mummy a fat cow. You're a silly slapper anyway because our mum told us.'

Oh no, it's world war three now and they've only just arrived!

Second week

Who nicked it? I want to know who stole my second week; have I been in a coma or something? It's not just me as I have spoken to numerous other holiday makers and they all say the same. The first week of your two week holiday goes like a dream and you thoroughly enjoy the slow relaxed atmosphere. Then, before you know what is happening, you are being collected by the coach in two hours. A week is a week isn't it? How can one week go so slowly and then another week fly by so fast?

Is it the tour operators who only give you ten days but tell you that it's a fortnight?

Sewing kits

Are you really going to start sewing on holiday? Forget it!

Shade stealers

You go onto the beach and pay for two sun beds plus an umbrella. So far so good, but you want to sit in the sun for a while in order to build up your tan so the umbrella can wait for a while. What happens? Some wassock sidles up and sits in the shade created by YOUR umbrella. That can't be right can it? It's a difficult one this, as who actually owns a piece of shade? The umbrellas are usually in a fixed position on the beach so you have two choices. You can either leave them alone (No way) or you can throw your towel down next to theirs and then gradually start nudging them over. What are you doing? You have a perfectly good sun bed to lie on and yet you are now lying on your towel on the beach. You shouldn't have to do that, so I would recommend either smacking them or just telling them to fffffff – 'please get out of my shade!'

Shell suits

Ha ha – phew!

I don't think shell suits have been available for sale for about thirty five years so how can it be that you still sometimes see British tourists walking around in them?

Shopping

If you arrive at your foreign holiday resort and you're staying in an apartment or if you want to sneak something into your hotel room because their prices are extortionate, then here are one or two grocery translations you should obtain and take with you for emergency supplies –

Beer
Bacardi
Cola
Gin
Tonic
Wine

There you go; you should be okay now!

Shorts (ladies)

As mentioned earlier in the book, it is quite fashionable these days for men to wear long shorts. Sometimes these shorts finish just above the knee and sometimes men prefer the ones that finish below the knee (see also Jelly Soldier). Certain ladies however, do not appear to follow this man fashion and prefer to wear short shorts. Many big fat ladies seem to wear VERY short shorts and they are the last people who should be wearing them. Why don't their husbands tell them that they look ridiculous? You can be walking along the sea front in any foreign tourist resort and there she is in front of you, 'Lard bottom'. She has a bum like a melted wellie and it's all hanging out of her shorts – yuk!

Shorts (travelling home)

Don't do that! You really do look like a proper idiot when you arrive back in the UK.

Shower gel

Is there a knack to it?

Many people (including myself) don't like shower gel and prefer to stick with a good old bar of soap. However, when going on holiday it's far more convenient to pack a bottle of shower gel than it is a bar of soap. The problem is that because we bar of soap users are not used to using shower gel, we waste 99% of the contents of the bottle. There must be a trick to it but I haven't mastered it yet and I don't think that I ever will. There should be more concise instructions on the bottle.

Into the shower I go once the water is running at the correct temperature, eyes closed and onto my hand goes the shower gel, slap, slap, rub, rub – nothing! I then open my eyes and look at my hands together with the places where I think that I have slapped the stuff. There's nothing there. Not a thing. It's all gone down the plug hole, I think?

I just can't do it. What a waste. Does it evaporate?

Showers

Many hotel rooms and apartments abroad only have a shower. If you want a bath then it's down to the sea or wait until you get home. Tough! This presents a problem to some men, but not me of course. You ladies may not know this, because it's something men don't normally share with their wives but, (according to my mate) men sometimes wee wee in the shower. I don't know what it is, but a man can have a wee wee before he gets into the shower and then, whilst under all that running water, he has to have another wee wee. In the shower! Yes. My mate and many other men are not particularly proud of it but they can't help it - apparently!

Showers (head back)

There is something different about having a shower whilst on holiday. I don't know why it is, but it's almost certainly the fact that you have been in the sun all day covered in sun tan cream or oil. You may even be half covered in sand if you have been on the beach. 'Ooooh, I can't wait to get back for a nice shower'. You feel dirty, sticky and getting into that shower is absolute heaven. You get the water temperature just right and climb in armed with all those exotically fragranced shower gels and shampoos - 'Aaah!' You're relaxed now, it's perfect, so you just stand there and let the hot water run all over you 'Aah - this is perfection.' Why is it though; I never have this problem at home and I have at least one shower if not two every day. It must be that I'm not as relaxed at home but I always do it on holiday. I stand there in the shower 'Aah' then for some unknown reason I put my head back as far as I can and open my mouth 'Aaaaaaargh, phloooooo, cough, splutter.' I have just swallowed two gallons of water and that tropical fruits shampoo which smelt great ten seconds ago now tastes like sulphuric acid – 'Aaaargh!'

Do you do that on holiday? If so why?

Side of the bed or nearest the door

It's just a 'decide as it happens' situation now, but many years ago I can remember going on holiday and when it was time to go to bed, Chris pulled back the sheet and got into the opposite side of the bed to which she normally sleeps.

'Hang on a minute, you don't normally sleep on that side of the bed'.

'I normally sleep nearest to the door'.

'Yes, but at home that's at this side of the bed, and I usually sleep at that side'.

'But I like to be nearest to the door'.

'Yes, but we're now the wrong way around in bed'.

I was totally confused!

I had always slept on the left side of the bed and I just assumed that was the way we (she) preferred to sleep. Never once did I realize it was because she liked to sleep nearest to the door.

Is that normal?

Sidle off the beach

'I'm just going for a stroll along the beach love' (see also Take away sandwiches). That's a proper lie and you know exactly where you are really going. Your wife is reading her book and you have spotted a beach bar about a hundred yards along. It looks really inviting and a stroll along the beach is an obvious exit line because as you get level with the bar your body automatically does a sharp turn and you sidle up the beach. An hour or so later, depending on how lucky you are, your wife wonders where the hell you have got to and she finds you in the bar. You say, 'Fancy that, I was walking along the beach when I spotted this place and thought I would just nip in for six, I mean a pint – hic.'

You're in trouble again!

Slavering

It is a fact of life that if you hire a sun bed on the beach abroad, you will invariably see someone nearby who has fallen asleep slavering. Is it you? If you watch carefully, it usually starts with a little twitch whilst asleep, then a low snore prior to the dispensing of liquid from the side of the mouth. Some people should bring a bib with them. How about one of those plastic Tommy Tippee children's type bibs with a trough at the bottom? Can you buy adult versions of those?

Slobber chops!

Slippers

If it's not the summer season, take your slippers on holiday with you abroad. Slippers are not going to be at the top of your 'I must bring them' list, but think about it. Out of the summer season abroad (depending on where you go), the evenings can get quite chilly and there are very few fitted carpets or central heating installations. Marble floors – your feet are cold. Bring the old slippers, they're a god send.

Your wife might look a bit of a dog in them, but at least her feet will be warm!

Snorkeling

Come on, admit it, I bet on one of your holidays you have seen people in the sea snorkeling and decided to give it a try. You go to the nearest souvenir type shop and buy a snorkeling mask and flippers don't you? You can't do it properly and you look like a proper twonker! I did it once when my son Oliver was around six or seven years old and what a carry on that was. Off we go then - on go the flippers and the mask next to the swimming pool. I couldn't breath properly, the glass steamed up, I was walking like a deformed duck and I must have looked like a proper one hundred percent retard. Oliver was bent in half laughing at me and there I was getting quite annoyed because I was trying to take it seriously. When I did eventually get (fall) into the water, I just sank and all the water came down that tube thing and then down my throat. I nearly killed myself. Try as I may, I couldn't do anything. There I go, splashing my arms around, kicking my legs and trying not to let the tube go under the water but I didn't go anywhere – sack that and get a pint! I still have a photograph somewhere and I look as though I have just got off a space ship from the planet Zogg. I looked worse because when I got my flippers back to the hotel and took them out of the bag, the shop had given me one orange flipper and one pink one.

I reckon I must have been the first ever punk rocker snorkeler!

Soaps

This is one thing which never ceases to amaze me, and its not just women who do it. Some people wait all year for their well earned holiday and then spend half of it in a bar watching soaps. You can go into virtually any British owned bar abroad and there they are, 'The Gawpers!' It can be blazing sunshine outside and there they all are watching Eastenders, Coronation Street or Emmerdale. Sometimes if they're in a sports bar with multiple TV screens, these people can be sat there with their heads shooting in all directions trying to watch them all at the same time. I have nothing whatsoever against this pastime, but I don't want to be involved in it thank you very much. The last thing I want if I walk into a bar on holiday for a drink is for soaps to be on the television. It's like being in a library but with selective noise only. They can have the TV volume on as loud as they like but if you dare to speak then you're wasted and verbally assassinated. 'Shhhhhh, tut tut, I wish he would shut up.' You get the lot.

Please do forgive me for speaking!

Can't you live without soaps for just a fortnight? No! Oh okay then.

Socks with sandals

The less said the better!

Sombreros

I've never seen a Spaniard in one yet! If you go to Spain for your holiday you've got to buy a sombrero haven't you? Loads of tourists buy them. Pink sombreros, purple sombreros, striped sombreros, extremely large mega sized sombreros. You name the colour and you can buy a sombrero in it.

I reckon sombreros are the best marketing idea ever. Brits go to Spain and buy a sombrero because they think they're Spanish when actually the Spanish don't even wear sombreros. They aren't very good for fitting into your suitcase either, so many tourists keep them on their heads on the flight home and boy, do they look like idiots or what? I want to know what tourists do with their sombreros once they get them home to the UK. I've never seen anyone in Tesco wearing a sombrero and I've never seen anyone driving a car wearing a sombrero.

Where do they all go – in the loft?

Speedo swimming trunks

I don't think so!

Spirit measures

'Wheeeeeeeeeeee – I think I'm wasted!' If you order a gin, whisky, Bacardi, vodka, or any other spirit for that matter in a foreign bar, you're in for a shock! It's a pleasant shock though because a spirit measure abroad is often at least a UK treble and sometimes approaching a quadruple. You think all of your birthdays have come at once, until you've had three or four and then you realize that you shouldn't have had the last one – then it's -

'What are you looking at?'

'Did you just call my vodka and tonic a puff?'

'That's my missus you're staring at.'

You're wrecked aren't you – again!

Squeeky mattresses and loose bed heads

It's extremely embarrassing!

I think it would be fair to say that couples tend to be a bit more amorous whilst on their holidays and that's fair enough. However, the combination of being amorous and the man having had eight pints can be very noisy indeed. Hotel and apartment mattresses tend to take a lot of hammer over a period of time and they sometimes squeak like hell. The bed heads are sometimes loose as well. This makes it quite obvious to the person in the next room or the room below (me) exactly what they're doing. Squeak, squeak, squeak squeak, squeak squeak squeak, squeaksqueaksqueaksqueaksqueaksqueak! He's on one now and there's no stopping him. What a racket. The problem is made worse by the fact that he's had eight pints and you know damn well that he's going to last for ages. He thinks he's a Grand National winner on Viagra.

There you are laid in bed with your wife or partner and there's a mini earthquake taking place next door. You look at her and she looks at you. You smile at each other; look away; look at each other again; roll your eyes; smile again; what should you do?

Have you had eight pints as well?

SSF

You must have had one of these SSF's in a foreign hotel - (**S**treaky bacon, **S**notty eggs and **F**rankfurters). That's not a proper breakfast! I take my hat off to foreigners; they do try to accommodate the Brits whenever they can, but they just cannot get the English breakfast right. It isn't difficult is it? You can go to one of the many British owned cafes along the sea front and get a perfectly good English breakfast because they usually use British suppliers for their bacon and sausages. Not the foreign hotel manager, oh no, he's used Paco's Spanish bacon and frankfurters for fifteen years. Strange that, because British tourists in his hotel have been leaving all their breakfasts for fifteen years.

I wonder if there's a connection?

Steak

If you are staying in a hotel then the chances are that you will eat in the hotel restaurant most, if not all of the time. If you are staying in an apartment however, then go to a local butchers shop and buy a couple of steaks. Its proper steak abroad, purplish and marbly. Steak from UK supermarkets doesn't taste of anything anymore – its rubbish! I have paid a fortune for a couple of fillet steaks in England and I could have been eating pork or chicken for all I knew. It looks appetizing because it's bright red, but it doesn't taste any different to the polystyrene tray it is sat in. There is a lot of Argentinean steak abroad and they actually hang the meat before they sell it to you. Buy some, it's a treat!

Sticky sun beds

Aren't some sun beds disgusting? Why don't the sun bed attendants hose them down every night? You like to think that it's sun tan cream and oil but it could be absolutely anything and you wouldn't know would you? Okay, you put your beach towel on the sun bed but at some point down the line you are then going to lay on it the other way around and the thought of that is yukky.

Other people's stickiness of all descriptions – whaaaaaa!

Sticky Vicky

It is many years since I saw Sticky Vicky in Benidorm and I'm told that her daughter does it now. Have you seen her? Wow, how does she do all that stuff? It's not normal is it? In my younger years I went out with all kinds of girls and I think it would be fair to say that some of them had been around the block a few times and had high mileage, but – pulling light bulbs out of there isn't right – is it? The first time I saw her I was near the back and I thought I must be seeing things. I had to go back early the following evening in order to sit near the front (not too near in case she picked on me). Light bulbs; there they were again. I hadn't been imagining it at all, light bulbs, keys; you name it – pulling them out of THERE! She then went on to fire ping pong balls out of her wobbly bits at tremendous velocity. Not just one, loads of them! She missed her way; she should be on the telly – what a gal! What made her decide to start practicing that stuff in the first place? I'm sure you don't just wake up in the middle of the night and think to yourself, 'I think I'll go downstairs, push a few light bulbs inside myself and then see if I can pull them out again – lit up!'

Go and see Sticky Vicky if she hasn't electrocuted herself. She's a very nice, talented lady.

Stiletto heels

How inconsiderate can you get? Surely even someone with only half a brain would realize that walking on a marble or ceramic floor in stilettos makes a hell of a racket and drives the people downstairs to distraction. Why do some women do that? Have you ever noticed if you have someone in the room upstairs wearing stiletto heels that the noise never appears to be coordinated? It doesn't sound as if they're walking properly; it's more of a scrape and a clump. Surely if a woman has been used to wearing stiletto heeled shoes for a number of years then she would know how to walk in them properly. Could we be misjudging women here? Could it be that the woman upstairs is really a cross dressing man? He could be up there with his girly dress, make up, a wig, and a huge pair of size thirteen stilettos on. That would explain things I guess. Next time you hear that racket from the room upstairs, run up and bang on the door shouting

'You sad pervert, put your flip flops back on.'

Then again, you might get a slap from a slapper!

Stub your toe

'Ow, ow, ******* ouch!' Us Brits are not used to walking around in sandals. Result? You can be walking anywhere; around your hotel room, on the beach, on the pavement, anywhere. Because you're not used to walking in sandals then you can't quite get the co-ordination right and you stub your toe on something. It hurts like hell and there are British tourists walking all over foreign tourist resorts shouting 'Ouch, Ow, *******, what the hell.'

Just listen next time you go!

Sudden stop

Once you have departed the aircraft and collected your suitcases, you walk out towards the main arrivals lounge and are usually part of a queue resembling a herd of sheep. This herd is finally channeled through a fairly narrow gate where all the throngs of friends and relatives are waiting to greet the travellers. What always happens? You want to get out of the airport as soon as humanly possible with your trolley full of suitcases but the idiots in front of you just stop dead. Why? Their friends or relatives have greeted them at the jaws of the gate into the arrivals lounge. They don't even think to carry on until they are in a position to let everyone behind them get through; oh no! They are stood there with their arms around each other saying things like 'Oh, great to see you' or 'Was it a good flight?' or 'You made good time didn't you?' What are these people on? They're holding up a couple of hundred people and they don't give a damn. Is it that they are incredibly inconsiderate? Is it that they just don't give a damn? Is it that they are just very relaxed laid back type people who don't think that anyone is in a rush?

Well I am! That's it; bang! Into the ankles goes the trolley. 'Oh dear, I'm ever so sorry.' Mallet head!

Sun bed orientation

Your first day around the pool is absolute heaven isn't it? You have waited all year for this holiday and once you arrive at your hotel you can't wait to dump the cases and get round that pool. On goes the swim suit together with the high factor sun cream and it's down to the pool for your first day – 'Hee hee – I can't wait!' You feel a little bit conspicuous because you're all white but what the hell, that will soon change. 'Quick, there are a couple of empty sun beds over there so let's leg it over and grab them'. It's late morning and these are the only sun beds available 'Phew – that was a bit of luck'. What happens at one or two o'clock in the afternoon just when you thought things couldn't get any better? The sun has moved around and your sun beds go into the shade – 'Aaaargh!'

That's why these sun beds were empty!

Sun bed vigilantes

I love these guys, they have me in stitches. You can sit on your balcony above the pool fairly early in the morning and watch them in action. They came on holiday to relax but in no time at all they are seriously rattled by the people who come down to the pool at seven o'clock in the morning in order to claim their sun bed and then go back upstairs to sleep. You can watch him; he's seriously worked up and on a mission. Up to the first sun bed, whip the towel off and then he's nearly into a run. Round the pool he goes throwing towels everywhere; into the bushes, into the pool, it doesn't matter where they go because all the people who have put towels onto a sun bed in order to claim it are complete morons to him. He's like Charles Bronson in Death Wish, but he wears shorts.

Sun bed vigilantes. They're great!

Sun glasses (Designer)

They're not real ones. Everyone at most foreign holiday resorts looks seriously rich because they wear very expensive designer sun glasses. Versace, Ray Bans, Mochinno, you name it. They cost next to nothing from the local lookie lookie man and they're actually a load of garbage. If you look anywhere near the sun you'll go blind.

They're not real ones you know!

Sun haters

If people hate the sun so much then why, oh why, do they go to countries with a hot climate for their holidays? How many times have you got into a conversation with someone on holiday and they come out with something like 'Oh it's hot here' or 'I can't stand this heat'. Is it me? What on earth are they thinking about? To make matters worse, these sun hating people usually dress as though they're going out to a dinner dance. They are wearing a suit, shirt and tie (if it's a man), braces and brogues. Sweat is pouring out of them and they hate the sun.

Possibly if they went down the road and bought a pair of flip flops, shorts and a straw hat, they might see things differently.

Sun tan creams and oils

Don't buy them in the UK and bring them with you, it's not worth it! Foreign sun tan creams and oils are fantastic and much cheaper than what you would pay at home. Don't forget that most of the brands you buy in the UK are advertised on the telly and manufacturers have to pay some famous slapper a fortune for being photographed lying on a beach with a fake tan.

For instance: there is a brand in Spain called 'Babaria' which is particularly good. Not a very good marketing move I'll grant you. Why would a company launch a brand with a name that sounds like Babba? It puts Brits off straight away doesn't it? 'I'm going down to the beach now, so I had better put some factor six Babba on my face.' Yuk!

Don't be put off by the name as it really is very good and much cheaper than what you would pay in the UK.

Sun umbrellas

As mentioned earlier in the book, you can pay an absolute fortune during your holiday renting a couple of sun beds and a sun umbrella. As such, in order to save some well earned money, some people just go to one of the local shops and buy one of those sun umbrellas with a spike at the bottom of the central rod which sticks into the sand. Now sand is not a particularly dense material for sticking something into and if there's only the slightest breeze then it's 'Let's all have a bloody good laugh time!'

Slight breeze – wobble wobble!

Slightly stronger breeze – wobble, lift a bit, wobble!

Sudden gust – Wheeeeeeeee! It's up in the air now and tearing down the beach at tremendous speed knocking the hell out of anyone in its path.

It is absolutely side splitting funny watching the person who owns this spikey brolly thingy legging it down the beach apologizing to everyone they pass. If the brolly is doing tipple tails along the beach then this person is petrified in case the pointy end skewers some innocent sun bather and they're up on a manslaughter charge.

Spikey sun umbrellas – it's worth buying one just for the exercise and the laugh!

Supermarkets (foreign)

Many men whilst on their foreign holiday volunteer to go to the supermarket. Why? Because there's a bar – wheeeeey! He clocked it on the first day when he went to the supermarket with his wife for the initial little shop and now he can't wait to run out of something. 'I'll go love, I don't mind, I could do with the walk.' Liar! Foreign supermarkets are great as there is usually a little cafeteria in the corner which sells beer. It can be half a day's job for a man buying a box of milk and a loaf of bread in these establishments. He absolutely hates shopping in the UK but somehow he has suddenly developed a fanatical passion for going to the foreign supermarket.

I wonder why?

Swapping addresses

You can get talking to another couple in a bar or on the beach and think nothing of it when all of a sudden these people think that you're their best mates in the whole wide world. On a couple of other occasions during your holiday you might bump into them again and have another chat. You hardly know these people and although they seem quite nice, that's about it. What happens next? 'It's been lovely talking to you and we have enjoyed your company so much. I'll just get a piece of paper and a pen so that we can exchange telephone numbers and addresses.' 'What – er – yes – er – okay then.' At this point you and your wife or partner are sat there with your mouths wide open and wondering how the hell you can get out of this one. Do you give them the wrong address and telephone number or just hope and pray that they lose it on the way home. Are they really going to contact you once you get home and arrange to come to your house or for you to visit their house? 'Oh no, I hope not.'

They're nice people, but what makes them think we like them so much?

Swimming pool wee wee

How many of you can honestly put your hand on your heart and swear to God that you have never had a wee wee in a swimming pool? Come on, be honest! I think you can split the general public into two distinct categories here. There are those who admit to having had a wee wee in a swimming pool at some point in their lives - and liars.

Which one are you?

Syrups (wigs)

You have to feel sorry for men who wear a syrup on holiday don't you? They can't go into the sea for a swim can they? I have never seen a wig sat on its own on a sun bed whilst the owner goes for a swim. If they did, all the other tourists would take the mickey when the guy came back and repositioned the syrup back on his head wouldn't they? Also, if the guy wears it all of the time whilst sun bathing, then when he gets back to the comfort of his hotel room he must look a right plonker when he takes it off. He has a white head when the rest of his body has a sun tan. Whilst on the subject, I reckon that all men who wear syrups must think that the rest of the population talk out of the side of their mouths. The reason I say that is the fact that most people I know say to their partners or mates, 'Look at that guys syrup', or 'Syrup at twelve o'clock'. People always say this out of the corner of their mouth so that the syrup wearer can't hear them.

Why is that?

T

Take away sandwiches

You're sat on the beach with your wife and possibly the children. Someone says 'I'm hungry' – yippee! At home the man would almost never volunteer to go to the shop but he's on holiday now and he would absolutely love to go for a couple of take away sandwiches. 'I'll go; I could do with a stroll'. He wants to go for the take away sandwiches because he knows he can have a pint whilst he is waiting. Once he's downed the pint he has the taste and orders another pint and then one for the road. When he finally gets back to the family I say (I mean he says), 'My God, they're slow in that place!'

Talking slowly to foreigners

It is a cast iron fact that most foreigners who live and work in foreign holiday resorts speak English. Many of them speak English fluently. Why is it then that us Brits speak to the fluent English speaking foreigners as though they're retarded. He may be a waiter in a restaurant or bar and he says to you in perfect English 'Hello, what can I get for you?' Your reply will inevitably be something like 'I - would - like - a - large - beer - please'. You look this person straight in the eye and speak very slowly to him. You exaggerate the mouth movement as if he's a child. He has already spoken to you in English which is as good as yours but you still do it.

It's a habit – I think?

Tattoos (Chinese/Japanese)

There is a definite trend at the moment for both men and women to have oriental symbols as tattoos. In the UK you don't notice them very much because they are usually covered up, but on a foreign beach you see lots and lots of people who have this oriental lettering tattooed on their shoulder, back, leg, or even their bum. What does it say? You don't know do you? Let's just say that you fancy one of these oriental tattoos so you go down to the local tattoo artist and ask him to put 'whatever' in Chinese on your left buttock. Even if the tattoo artist in question just happens to speak Chinese, which I think is highly unlikely, then it doesn't mean to say that he will tattoo what you have asked for onto your buttock does it? I think that tattoo artists probably have a terrific sense of humour and it wouldn't surprise me in the least if there aren't women walking about thinking they have some profound oriental wording on their buttocks when, in reality, it could actually say 'LARD XXXX' or 'YOU PAID ME A FORTUNE FOR THIS – IDIOT'. The lady wouldn't know would she?

If you do decide to get one of these oriental tattoos, go down to your local Chinese take away afterwards and flash the cheek of your bottom asking them what it says!

Tattoos (on older women)

Yuk yuk yuk! Men have had tattoos for years and years and years, even going back to pirate times. Sailors in particular have always been big tattoo fans. These days, however, many young women have tattoos and these young women will shortly become middle aged and older women.

Guffaw guffaw - say no more!

Taxi fares

Beware the foreign taxi fare! Many, if not most foreign taxis do not have a meter on the dash board. In fact they don't have a meter at all. What they do have is a tatty sheet of paper in the glove box which tells the driver how much to charge you for the distance he has travelled. Of course you don't see the writing on this piece of paper so you haven't got a clue whether he is charging the correct price or not. In most cases he isn't. You can get a foreign taxi every night for a week from the same pick up point to the same destination and you will be charged a different price every night.

They're having a laugh – aren't they?

Taxi suicide airport runs

Oh Chriiiiiiiiiiiiiiiiiist! I'm on holiday, so what's the rush? Most of these foreign taxi driver guys must qualify for their licence by taking part in the Le Mans twenty four hour race. They're complete lunatics. It's not too bad in and around your holiday resort but a taxi ride to or from the airport is serious suicide stuff. I know that the more fares these guys do in a day the more they earn, but come on; it's not worth dying for. Even if he doesn't value his own life, then you would think that he would consider his passengers. No!

Tell him to slow down. Don't be afraid; just tell him. Who's paying anyway!

Temperature

When you see the temperature at a particular foreign place or resort in British newspapers, it has usually been taken in the shade. Also, when they give you the temperature on the radio or on the TV, it's been taken in the shade. Why do they do that? If you or I go on holiday then we sit in the sun don't we? You could be laid there in the sun thinking its seventy five degrees and comfortable when in actual fact it's ninety degrees and you're burnt! Why don't they do what they do with foreign currency rates where they give a business rate and a tourist rate? They could give a 'shade' temperature and a 'tourist' temperature so that we would all know where the hell we stood. Tourists aren't really bothered what the temperature is in the shade as they sit in the sun; otherwise they may as well stay at home.

Come on weather people – we want 'sun' temperatures as well please!

Ten past two

Ten past two in the afternoon that is. Avoid any roads like the plague. Many shops and businesses abroad close at two o'clock in the afternoon in order for their staff to go home and have a little siesta. The problem is that most of them don't just live around the corner so the roads are absolutely mental between two and half past in the afternoon. They're desperate to get home for a little kip and will gladly run you over during the proceedings because they only have a couple of hours.

Careful! Ten past two is dangerous.

Terrorists

Is there one on my flight?

You do it don't you; look at other people in your check-in queue? 'He looks a bit shady, is that a gun in his pocket or is he just excited because he's going on holiday?' You look at his feet in order to see if he's wearing exploding shoes. You then look at his baseball cap to see if you can see the outline of a grenade inside it. Poor fella – he's probably a very very nice man.

On the other hand?

Text messages (to you)

'Where the hell has all my credit gone? I haven't even sent a text or phoned anyone yet.'

If you take your mobile telephone with you on your foreign holiday and it is 'pay as you go', be careful! Make sure the credit is well topped up because you can be two or three days into your holiday with your mobile for emergency use only, when all of a sudden the credit is eaten before you know what's happened. You have only received two texts from your children and one from a friend. The credit's gone! If and when someone in the UK sends you a text message or phones you then YOU pay most of the cost. That can't be right can it? Why should you pay for someone else's desire to contact you? If you wanted to contact them then that's fair enough, but come on, the mobile telephone companies are taking the mickey aren't they? If you take your mobile telephone on holiday, take the chip out until YOU want to text or phone someone!

Pay for your call and not theirs. That's fair enough isn't it?

Toilet paper in the bin

Come on: that's just not right is it?

There are a number of holiday destinations where the waste pipes are a much smaller diameter than they are in the UK. Now, I have got to be desperately desperate to go for a number two whilst I am out anywhere, never mind on holiday. It's at my own place or nowhere, that's it. Nevertheless, sometimes one is taken short and there's only one thing for it and that's to go into a bar or café if you're not within striking distance of your own accommodation. 'Ooooh, aaaaargh – just made it'. You sit down or hover just above the seat and then you see it; the sign. 'Do not put toilet paper down the toilet. Put your used toilet paper in the bin provided' (It's usually spelt wrong). Come on; their having a laugh aren't they? No! I don't know about you but I just can't do it, it's not right. The thought of lifting that bin lid and looking at someone else's toilet paper is a bridge too far for me, but it's just as bad thinking that someone else will then look at my toilet paper. Sack that. It's straight down the toilet and to hell with dodgy plumbing.

It's not right; it can't be, can it?

Toilet seats in hotels

They do it in the UK as well. The cleaner puts a length of printed tape around the toilet seat which is, I think, to prove that it's been cleaned. It doesn't prove a thing does it? All it proves is that someone has put a length of printed tape around the toilet seat.

Really useful that is!

Towed away

If you hire a car whilst you are on holiday abroad, be careful where you park. Remember that the street signs are in a foreign language and the chances are that you won't have a clue what they say. Many legitimate parking spaces have set times during the day when they can only be used for loading and unloading. If you don't realize that, then your car will be gone when you return. If there is a line of cars illegally parked then your hire car will always go first. It is a cast iron fact that when the tow truck arrives it will pull the foreign plated and hire cars away first. The locals cars will be left as foreigners look after their own. That's a fact!

Talking about having your car towed away reminds me that we had our VW Beetle towed away once in Fuengirola. I parked in what I thought was a legitimate parking place, as there were no yellow lines in sight, but what I hadn't noticed were the large wheelie bins on the pavement nearby. When Chris and I came back, the car was gone, and there was only one explanation: the tow truck. Of course, it could have been stolen, but that seemed highly unlikely, bearing in mind its colour.

I went round to the local police station and told them that I thought our car had been towed away, and we had the following conversation – in Spanish, which left me at somewhat of a disadvantage, as my Spanish wasn't very good at the time.

'What kind of car is it?' asked the policeman behind the desk.

'Er, er.' I didn't know what the word for beetle was in Spanish. 'It's um, well; it's er…'

'What kind of car is it?' he asked again, a little less sympathetically.

I did know what the word for cockroach was, so I just went with that. 'Cucaracha,' I said firmly.

The policeman glanced down involuntarily at the floor and then turned to look behind him. Relieved at seeing no cockroaches, and obviously starting to get a bit annoyed, he asked again.

'What kind of car is it?'

'It's a cucaracha – a Volkswagen cucaracha'.

Suddenly the penny seemed to drop. 'Ah, si. What colour is it?'

Oh hell, this was going to be difficult. You may have seen a new-shaped Volkswagen Beetle in the same colour as ours. You'll certainly remember if you have, because it's the most stupid colour you've ever seen in your life. I think its official name is actually 'lime yellow', which just about sums it up: it's not green and it's not yellow; it's somewhere in the middle. But I had no idea what 'lime yellow' was in Spanish.

'It's not green and it's not yellow,' I said, helpfully.

'Well what colour is it then?' the policeman asked, speaking slowly and clearly.

'It's sort of green and sort of yellow.'

It was obvious that his patience was wearing thin. 'So, is it green or is it yellow?'

I decided it was time to make a decision. 'Er, er – yellow,' I said.

'Okay, yellow. Now, what is the registration number?'

We still had our British registration at the time, which was AJO – which means 'garlic' in Spanish. Whenever we stopped at a zebra crossing or traffic lights, people would stare in amazement at the colour – which isn't available in Spain – and then start laughing when they noticed the number plate. Nervously, I spelled it out.

The policeman stood up and leaned towards me across the counter, and for a fleeing moment the thought crossed my mind that he was going to nut me on the forehead. But with his face about an inch from mine, he just glared at me and then sat back down and repeated his question.

'What's the registration number?'

I told him again, and I think it crossed his mind to arrest me for taking the mickey, or else to breathalyse me, but, thankfully, he obviously decided to give me the benefit of the doubt.

We got the car back, although in some respects it might have been good if it had been stolen, so that we'd have been able to replace it with a white car with registration letters that meant nothing in any language.

Train in a petrol station?

(See also Wally Trolley). Have you seen these train things going around foreign tourist resorts which aren't real trains? They're tractor type thingies which are made to look like trains and they have trailers behind them which carry tourists around the resorts. I once pulled into a petrol station in southern Spain in order to fill my car up with petrol and there it was, parked at a petrol pump, a train!

I hadn't had a drink - but I thought that I had!

Transvestites

I don't know anything about transvestites – honest! However, whilst writing this book and thinking about different things that happen on holiday and the different people who go on holiday, for some strange reason I started to wonder about transvestites. How often do they do it? Dress up like girlies I mean. When transvestites go on holiday, do they bring all their gear with them? Can they wait for a week or two before putting the sussies on? They can't win I guess. If the hotel staff and/or other guests know that a man is staying in room number so and so and then all of a sudden a woman walks out who has a huge Adams apple, then the cover is blown, so to speak! They'll take the mickey out of him. Sorry, but that's the way it is. If, on the other hand, this person is stopped at customs and his suitcase is searched – oops! Explain that away then! You can picture a customs officer lifting a frilly thong, suspender belt, ankle length dress and stillettos out of his case and the person concerned saying something like, 'My niece lives in Italy and she can't get things like this.'

Yea right!

Travel irons

What are they all about? Some of them weigh more than your suitcase. I can understand that some people are so obsessed about their appearance that they like to have freshly ironed clothes, but is it completely necessary to have a razor type crease in your Bermuda shorts? If you didn't take the big stupid travel iron then you would have the extra weight for lots more clothes.

What is it that makes some people think that it's completely necessary to take an iron on holiday with them? Is it me?

TV

Don't believe what you are told or what you read!

If your travel agent tells you that there will be a TV in your hotel room or if it states in your travel brochure that there's a TV, it's only partly true. There will be a TV and it will work, but the channels available will be mostly useless to you. It will be foreign TV which you will not understand and in all likelihood the best you will get is CNN News.

If it states that you will have a TV in your room then don't get excited about being able to watch your favourite programmes. Because you won't!

Two mates

Do you do it? I do, and I can't help it. If I see two blokes on holiday together then I automatically assume that they are gay. I don't make the same assumption if I see two women together. Why is that? It's not fair really and I'm sure that in most cases this assumption is completely and utterly wrong.

Is it just me; is it a blokey thing?

u

Umbrella hats

Have you seen them abroad? The lookie lookie men and gift shops sell them and they are completely and utterly knobby. They're like a miniature umbrella but instead of a stick underneath it there's a rim which you sit on your head. Why on earth would anyone want to walk around on holiday with a brightly striped miniature umbrella stuck on their head? Okay, you could say that they are very practical in order to keep the sun off your head but - come on! Do people buy and wear them so that other people will look at them and laugh? If so, then they are spot on correct, but people are not looking and laughing at them because they're really side slapping comical people. They're looking and laughing at them because they look like a complete retard.

On the other hand, you're on holiday so why not?

Vest type sleeveless T-shirts

Why is it that whenever you see a man on holiday wearing one of those vest type sleeveless t-shirts, he doesn't walk, he struts? They're like peacocks. They needn't be body builder type blokes either. He can be a fat sweaty bloke with a huge gut or a five stone weedy type bloke; but he still struts.

Do they think they look hard wearing a vest on holiday? If so, why?

Village idiots

It's not a nice thing to say but, come on, when you're on holiday you come across some tourists who were definitely short changed in the brain department. They're a couple of clowns short of a circus aren't they? There is nothing physically or mentally wrong with these people in the true medical sense, but they're just daft! They walk around with their mouths half open, gawping at things which are of no interest whatsoever to anyone else, and usually trip over things.

Where do they come from and what do they do when they're not on holiday?

Waiters

Who's paying anyway?

Why is it that when you go into many foreign restaurants or hotel restaurants, the waiter appears to think that he is part of the aristocracy and that you are a piece of dog poo? I can't understand it, it's not right. In virtually any other kind of service industry it is the norm' to be nice and polite to customers, but these guys appear to believe that the more unhelpful they are to you, then the bigger the tip you will give them. Wrong! If they genuinely hate their job so much then they should get the hell out and become an undertaker or work for the local tax authorities.

The only tip he'll get from me is the tip of my boot. Twonker!

Wally trolley

I'm sure that you have already seen a Wally Trolley on your previous foreign holidays (see also Train in a petrol station). Wally Trolley is the name affectionately given by Brits who live abroad to those trains which travel around foreign holiday resorts showing the tourists the sights. They're not proper trains, just tractor things which are made to look like trains with trailers on the back where the tourists sit. Next time you are on one of those things and you see someone pointing at you, they're almost certainly calling you a Wally. I wonder if anyone has ever been run over by a Wally Trolley? Can you imagine the trouble you would have explaining it away to the police or the insurance company?

'I was just walking down the road when a train ran me over.'

'Yea right – have you been drinking?'

If you do get run over by a Wally Trolley, just say 'I was walking down the road when a Wally Trolley ran me over.' That's much more understandable!

Water management

In hot foreign climates they can go for literally months on end without any rain whatsoever. A total lack of rain is bad enough but on top of that the temperature during those hot summer months is constantly pushing up to and above thirty degrees centigrade. Wouldn't you think that by putting those two factors together there would be a drought the likes of which the world has never seen before? No! You can drive past golf courses abroad which look like billiard tables and there is water spraying out in all directions. There are people constantly getting showers on the beach, roundabouts which look like the hanging gardens of Babylon, trucks washing the streets with water, fountains spewing water all over the place and yet there's no rain. Water management – foreigners are fantastic at water management and they should send a few of them to the UK.

Now, just for a moment, imagine it not raining in Britain for a few months. Forget the fact that the weather in Britain is usually – well, er, crap actually, but there would be stand pipes in the streets and total panic everywhere. The reservoirs would be completely empty and people would be panic buying bottled French water.

How can it be?

Foreigners have red hot temperatures and hardly any rain whereas the British have rubbish weather and it rains most of the time. Who is it that has a water shortage first? The British! Certain arrogant Brits whilst visiting hot countries sometimes make comments along the lines of it being only one step up from third world, but come on – think about it! Certain areas of Britain can go for only two or three weeks without rain and there are hosepipe bans announced. Possibly the British water authorities should try and poach a few foreign water management people but why the hell would they want to go and live in a rubbish climate. Actually it's probably a good job they don't go over to Britain because if they did as good a job in Britain as they do in their own countries then many parts of the UK would be permanently under water!

Foreign water managers – Wow, respect!

British water managers – Ha ha ha – guffaw guffaw!

Water retention

Many people go on holiday and know for a cast iron fact that they are overweight. You can listen to holiday makers talking and saying things like, 'I'm not as fat as this at home' or 'It's not fair as I'm normally quite slim, but this heat makes me look fatter due to water retention'.

Oh, okay then. Anything you say!

Welcome parties

They should be called wakes!

If you go on a package holiday you will usually be invited to a 'Welcome Party' once you arrive at your hotel or apartment complex. These usually take place on the first morning following your arrival and you will be promised a free glass of Sangria, wine, beer or soft drink. People usually start wandering in looking a bit sheepish and taking their places as far away from the front as possible so as not to feel intimidated by the rep. They go through the usual gist about the resort, tell you where it's best to eat and drink (because they get a discount for doing so) and generally bore you to death in a monotone voice. They then try to sell you a few excursions or a drunken night out at some naff restaurant in the hills. Then comes the best bit; 'Does anyone have any questions or queries'. If you arrived at your hotel or apartment the previous day then there's a fair chance that you will have found something to complain about and that's when the rep suddenly loses interest. She asks the question and then you can almost see her face screw up as she prays there are no questions because she just can't be bothered sorting out your problems.

There must be some good holiday reps, but I have to say that I've never met one.

Chris and I were once staying in an apartment in the Canary Islands and when we arrived during the afternoon, we fancied a cup of tea. There wasn't a kettle so I part filled a small pan, turned on one of the electric rings, and placed the pan on the ring – ZZZZZZZZZZZZZZZZ – 'What the hell!' The pan handle was metal and what seemed to me like six million volts shot up my right arm. There was obviously some kind of short in the ring which made anything coming into contact with it live. So: as you would, I mentioned it at the welcome party. I swear to God that the holiday rep said to me 'Couldn't you wear some rubber soled shoes when you want to use the cooker.' Now come on, is she taking the mickey. I asked her if she was being serious and she confirmed that she was. I just flipped and Chris was holding onto me as if she thought I was going to jump up and punch her. I then replied, 'I haven't got any rubber soled shoes with me, but what if I wear a condom every time I want a cup of tea and push the pan onto the electric ring with my willy. Would that be okay?' She told me not to be sarcastic and to this day I cannot understand why?

Another example of the holiday rep was a friend of mine who was taken badly with a dodgy stomach on the first evening of his holiday at a hotel in Rimini. He managed it down to the Welcome Party the next morning but sat as near to the door as possible in case he had to leg it to the toilet. He wanted to question the other guests about their stomachs from the night before and sure enough, there were a few other sufferers. Having been made aware of this from the 'Any questions' bit at the end of the meeting, the rep asked what these people had eaten in the hotel restaurant on their first night. As it happened, all the poorly ones had eaten a pasta chicken dish. Armed with this earth shattering information, the following words of wisdom then came out of the holiday reps mouth, 'I wonder if you've caught that bird flu that's going around?'

You couldn't make it up. Welcome parties – shove 'em!

'What are you doing here?'

Has it ever happened to you on holiday - what kind of a question is that? You can be walking down a tiny street in a Spanish village or sitting on the terrace of a restaurant in Athens when someone will tap you on the shoulder and say 'What are you doing here?' It's someone you know from the UK and they want to know what you are doing there. You should say, 'I've come all the way over here in order to buy a nuclear submarine. What the hell do you think I'm doing here?'

'What have you done with the weather then?'

This has happened to me lots and lots of times and I'm sure that it has happened to you as well. I have possibly nodded to someone in my hotel or said 'Good Morning' to them once. I wake up one morning and the weather is poor. I am then walking through reception and this person says to me 'What have you done with the weather then?' Eh, are they talking to me? I don't have the ability to change the weather in any way whatsoever, but if I did I certainly wouldn't make it rain on my well earned holiday would I?

Do people say that to you – 'What have you done with the weather then?' Are they being serious?

What should I take?'

'I haven't worn most of these clothes and shoes. Why on earth did

I bring this lot?' You do though don't you? It's not just women either. Once it gets close to your departure date you start thinking about what clothing you will require for your holiday. Depending on what time of year you are going and where you are going to, it can be very difficult indeed. There you are in the UK freezing your wotsits off and it's almost impossible to comprehend that it's hot and sunny where you are going. Best play safe though eh? Two pullovers, socks (tights), a leather jacket, four pairs of shoes, possibly a raincoat?

I bet that most UK tourists who go on holiday to the sun don't even wear half of what they take. I know I don't!

'What time is it?'

You lose track of time on holiday don't you? You ask that question literally hundreds of times because more often than not, you don't have a watch on. That's a good sign. If you don't know what time it is then you're relaxed and that's why you came on holiday in the first place.

Mission accomplished!

'What day is it?'

Unlike 'what time is it', this one can have a number of different explanations. If you don't know what day it is then it can mean that you are really, really, really, really relaxed, and that's fantastic. On the other hand, if you don't even know what day it is then the chances are that you are either completely and utterly legless or just recovering from being completely and utterly legless.

Which one are you then?

'What's that smell?'

When you get off the plane at your holiday destination airport abroad there is a unique smell and I don't know what it is? It's

191

not a pleasant smell, but then again it's not an unpleasant smell either. There is the immediate blast of heat that hits you when you are in the foreign fresh air but there's that smell as well. What is it? Is it humidity? Is it the heat? I haven't got a clue what it is, but I'm sure you know what I mean.

Or is it just me?

White slip on shoes (men)

Usually with white socks and half mast trousers! You bought those in the 70's together with that belt with the big shiny buckle didn't you? It's time for a change now pal. They may have looked okay in the 70's but to be honest, you look a bit of a twonker in them now.

Bin them!

White stripes

Have you ever noticed whilst on holiday that women in strappy dresses never raise their arms during the evening? It's because people get a sun tan, but for some unknown reason they can never get a sun tan down the sides of their body from under the armpit to just above the waist. They look stupid and they know they look stupid so they keep their arms down by their sides. It doesn't matter really because everyone else is in the same boat with white stripes running down the sides of their body, but ladies do it all the same. It's like watching a wildlife programme in the bar because women in strappy dresses walk to the toilet or for another drink like a penguin. Wobble wobble, 'Mustn't lift my arms', wobble wobble, 'because I've got white stripes running down the sides of my body'.

She makes a mental note to sunbathe with her arms out to the sides or above her head tomorrow but it never works. White stripes – always!

Wobble wobble!

White swim suits

Don't buy a white swim suit unless you have no intention of going into the water. If you do buy a white swim suit and you do go into the water, it gets wet and – erm – well; just don't do it eh?

'Who packed the cases?'

When a man arrives at his holiday destination and finds something missing from his case he always says 'So and so is missing; who packed the cases?' He knows damn well who packed the cases and it certainly wasn't him. Men don't do case packing so why is he asking 'Who packed the cases?' He can't be bothered to pack his own case but if something is missing then it's his wife's fault!

Seems fair enough to me!

Who's the boss in your house then?

I think it's embarrassing! Hen pecked men on holiday who have to ask their wife's permission to speak in public. You don't notice it as much at home in the UK as obviously you don't visit restaurants and bars as frequently. Sometimes the guy isn't even allowed to decide what he wants to eat or drink.

'I think I'll have a beer.'

'No you can't have a beer, it's too early.'

'Oh, okay love, I'll just have a coke then.'

'No; too much sugar in that, you know you must cut down on your sugar.'

Why, why, oh why, pray tell me, does he put up with it? Most women know better. Most women know damn well that if they **TELL** their husband or partner that he can't have a beer then in all probability he will have eight pints and then fall over. He (I) wouldn't do it to be nasty, but there is a huge difference between asking and **TELLING**. I know divorce is expensive, but to hell with the money. Order a pint anyway and then pour it over her head!

You've ordered a beer but you haven't drank it, so that should be alright shouldn't it?

WHY?

Why does my upper chest always go red in the sun instead of brown? Does yours? I have had this affliction for the whole of my life, a permanently red upper chest which refuses to change colour in the sun. When I was younger my mum used to tell me that it was a 'strawberry chest', and that it was a good thing to have because the film star Robert Mitchum had one. So what – what's that got to do with the price of fish? I can sunbathe for as long as I like; turn reddish, then brownish, then brown. But look at my upper chest, it does look like a strawberry actually, it also looks stupid.

I wonder if my mum ever went out with Robert Mitchum?

Why can't foreigners make tea?

I think it is fair to say that you can go into just about anywhere in the UK and get a decent cup of tea. Why is then that when you go on holiday it's downright impossible to get even a half decent cup of tea in a foreign hotel or café? They genuinely haven't got a clue, as I'm sure that they don't give you a cup of jollop on purpose. Okay, they don't have English tea bags but surely a tea bag is a tea bag is a tea bag isn't it? In most places you don't even get a tea pot as I don't think they've been invented abroad yet. The water isn't even boiling! They appear to pull hot water from a coffee machine type thingy which looks like a Dalek and then chat to a few mates for a couple of minutes. Into the cup of water goes the crappy tea bag as an afterthought, and what do you get – jollop! You can stir this stuff until the bottom of the cup wears out but it still won't give you anything resembling tea. On top of all of that, you then have to fish the tea bag out of the cup and the waiter gives you one of his special 'tosser' looks because you dribbled on his table cloth.

Tea abroad – it's naff!

Wobbly wheels

You have to do this; you must have fallen for it at least once already.

Before you pack your suitcase, take it out onto your drive and pull it along for ten or twenty feet. You will look like a complete and utter nutter to your neighbours I'll grant you, but it's worth it. Has your suitcase developed wobbly wheels? If it has, then buy a new one immediately as you know damn well that when you get to the airport or when you get off the transit coach at your hotel, everyone else will think that you're drunk. You're okay, but your suitcase has got a jive bunny inside it and makes you walk like a duck. You can pretend to laugh as much as you like and point to the case as though it has just adopted you, but to everyone else – you're wasted!

Bin it!

Women's white dresses

Why do women always save their tight fitting white dress until the end of their holiday? This is a very strange phenomenon, but it's true that many women save their tight fitting white dress until the end of their holiday because they assume that they will have cultivated a nice tan by that time and it will show the white dress off at its best. There's only one problem with that theory – it doesn't fit! During your holiday you have eaten well, probably drank a lot, and the heat has expanded your little bits of blubber.

Back in the case with the tight fitting white dress - again!

Wooden pegs

There aren't any abroad! If you are lucky enough to get a few pegs on your balcony for those little pieces of washing you may have, they will inevitably be plastic ones. The sun makes them brittle and they snap as soon as you look at them. Foreign gypsies mustn't be able to make proper wooden pegs so take a few of your own – you'll need them!

Xylophones

Leave yours at home. There are enough foreigners over there walking around bars annoying everybody with the stupid bloody things!

Yawning

You don't have to be on holiday to notice this because everyone knows that if you yawn and someone else sees you, then they in turn yawn. Conversely, if you see someone yawn, then the chances are that you will yawn. God knows why, it's just a fact. Just for a laugh; if you are lying on your sun bed on holiday and make a big deal out of pretending to yawn, then look up the line of sun beds. You can watch other people yawning in turn – it's like synchronized yawning.

Go on, try it, it's a laugh!

FINALLY – What about when you get home? Yuk!

Burglars

There haven't been any have there? You can have ten alarm systems, the neighbours going in every day, you could even have armed guards and a machine gun nest on your roof, but you think about it lots of times whilst you're on holiday don't you? *'I hope we haven't been burgled'.* You can be sat on the beach nodding off when all of a sudden you sit bolt upright – aaargh – you have visions of a man in a black and white striped t-shirt with a little black mask over his eyes and a swag bag over his shoulder rummaging around your house. You are so relieved when you get home and see that the house is perfectly okay.

Its normal - I think?

Chinese laundry

Once you get home you reluctantly empty the cases and it would be fair to say that you're more than a little naffed off. You're dreading going back to work but once that first working day is over and done with you're looking forward to getting home and having a nice relaxing evening and getting back to normal. You can't get in the front door. What the hell? When you do finally manage to open the door your whole house appears to be full of clothes. Clothes to wash, clothes to iron - your wife has had the lot out of the cases and your house looks like a Chinese laundry.

Sack that – I'm off down the pub!

Clocks go back!

The worst possible time to go away on your holiday is October. Why? Because as soon as you get back home the clocks go back and it's dark around half past four in the afternoon. You go to work in the dark and you get home from work in the dark. A few days ago you were sat on a foreign beach in the sun and life couldn't have been much better. But now, oh now, you feel that it would be a good idea if you went into hibernation for six months or so.

Suicide sounds pretty good!

Cold water – brrrrrrrr!

This is one of the first things you notice once you get back into your own home in the UK. You never notice it at all for the rest of the year but when you first get home from your summer holiday you turn the cold tap on in order to rinse your hands or face and its – 'Aaaargh, brrrrrrrr – the water's freezing.' Whilst abroad the cold water tap doesn't actually deliver cold water because the ground is warm where the water pipes are and it isn't what us Brits would call 'proper cold'. It's a shock when you get home.

Never mind; after a couple of goes it's well forgotten.

Dead skin in your socks

It's horrible isn't it? You get home with a nice tan and walk around as proud as hell for about three days. Then you develop leprosy! It doesn't matter how much cream you put on in the morning and before you go to bed, it doesn't take long. You get home from work on the third or fourth evening, take your socks off (if you're a man), and it starts snowing dead skin. Yuk, yuk, yuk!

Down to my local pub

Everyone's still here; sat and stood in the same place they were when I left for my holiday two weeks ago! Have I been in a time warp? Did I really go on holiday or was it all just a wonderful dream? The barmaid is wearing the same clothes; surely she must have been changed at least once during two weeks – probably not! There's old Geoff. He's complaining about all the single mothers, which is exactly what he was complaining about when I left two weeks ago. Dire Straits are still on the juke box and that's what was on when I left. Hell, this is unreal. Look over there; it's Harry and Margaret, sat in the corner with a barley wine each which is exactly where and what they were doing when I left two weeks ago - aaaaargh!

You never realized before, but for the other fifty weeks of the year when you're not on holiday, you do exactly the same as them in your spare time – 'Nothing'. Quick, leg it back down to the travel agents as you've got to get out of there and have something to look forward to.

'Is this all there is?'

Drive to work on the first day back – it's scary!

'Oh, I'm depressed and I'm in a foul mood. I know damn well what's waiting for me when I get into work. A huge backlog of work that's what. That lazy so and so who is supposed to cover for me won't have done a thing. I'll get my own back on him/her when they go on holiday though'. You're chuntering to yourself in the car before you have even arrived at work. What's wrong with you?

Back to reality. The holiday feeling soon disappears doesn't it?

First bath

You've had a fantastic holiday but there is something very special about your first bath at home. You could have had a hundred baths on holiday and it was probably a very nice bathroom in your accommodation, but it's not quite the same is it?

'Ooooh – phew – aaaah – my own bath!'

First day back at work

Once you actually get to work on that first day it's – 'Aaaaaaaaaaaaaarrrrrrrrgh' – what an absolute bummer! You want to be back at work on that first day about as much as you want to contract a terminal illness. The problem is that most of us realize that if we didn't go to work then we wouldn't have had a holiday in the first place. It just has to be done. What do you get when you arrive? All day long on that first day back – 'Did you have a nice holiday?' 'Yes thanks' or 'Great thanks' – boring, boring, boring. It would be much more realistic to hang a piece of cardboard around your neck saying something like, 'My holiday was naff, so don't ask!'

First night back

What do you do on your first evening back home? As soon as they open, you're straight down to the chippy or the local take away aren't you? You can't wait can you – yum yum!

First night back in your own bed

As with your first bath – 'Ah ooh ah' – that's great! Chris absolutely always changed the bedding prior to us going on holiday and it's a fantastic feeling climbing into your own fresh bed when you get home from your holiday – ooh!

Fitted carpets

They really do feel strange when you get home after walking on marble tiles in bare feet for two weeks. It doesn't feel right does it? Until tomorrow that is, when the holiday is well forgotten!

Haircut

'Ha ha ha – look at that plonker.' Are they talking about me? If you go for a haircut shortly after returning from your foreign holiday, then yes, they probably are talking about you. Why? Because you now have a sun tanned face and neck and – erm – a bright white border running all around your hairline – 'Pheeeeew, ha ha.' You look as though you have been down to the local car paint shop and asked them to coach line your face!

Hoping the people who asked for your telephone number don't contact you

We hardly knew them anyway. They were nice people but I sure hope that they don't phone us because we don't really want to be their best mates!

I've got to mow the lawn

Is it just me or am I particularly sad? I have had a great holiday but as soon as I board the plane on the way home, I'm on a mission to mow the lawn. If there has been a lot of rain the grass will be at least two feet high and I can't wait to cut it. If it's raining on our first day back then I won't be able to mow the lawn. 'Oh God, what will I do if I can't cut the grass?' That will be a complete disaster and I'm getting stressed out about the lawn before we are even in the air.

I guess I am sad!

Mail

'Oh no, I can't open the front door because there's a shed load of mail behind it'. When you do eventually climb over all this stuff you want to leave it until tomorrow, but you can't can you? You're then in a bad mood because as you sort through it you know for a fact that ninety percent will be junk mail and the other ten percent will be bills.

Welcome home!

Neighbour you hate

'Oh no, I forgot all about that low life idiot'. Whilst you have been away on your wonderful holiday you never even once thought about that nauseating neighbour of your. Who is the first person you see when you get back home? Yes – it's him (or her). You immediately give them the daggers and they then give you the daggers, so it's back to normal then?

Who's got the sun tan though; not them. Ner ner ner!

Someone else is just going

It's bad enough returning home from your holiday in the sun, but many UK airport designers appear to want to rub it in big style.

Some UK airports are designed in such a way that once you have left the plane you then walk down corridors towards the baggage collection area. As you are walking down this corridor feeling fairly depressed, who's coming towards you in the opposite direction laughing their heads off?

People who are just going on their holiday – aaaargh!

Sulk

Why not? Most of us do when we get home!

UK passport control

'Wow – I forgot just how polite some people can be in the UK.' You walk from the plane down to passport control prior to collecting your baggage. You're in the UK now and what does the passport control person do? He or she usually smiles at you! That's a real novelty compared to that foreign wassock who always gives me one of his special plonker looks.

Where's the sea?

Who nicked it? When you wake up on your first morning back at home you yawn, open the bedroom curtains, and it's 'Oh bugger, where's the sea? Yesterday when I did this I had the beautiful sea in my face and now all I can see is the arse end of a factory!'

Yodel to the dog when you collect it from the kennels

Why is it that people don't talk in the same voice to their dog as they do to other people? It's hard to write down what I mean, but I'm sure that you understand what I'm talking about. Your voice turns into a sort of high pitched yodel – *'Hello Rex, have you missed us? Have you been a good boy then?'* You haven't yodeled for a fortnight but it just comes out automatically once you collect your dog from the kennels or from a friend who has been looking after it.

'*Come to Mummy (or Daddy). Have you missed us? Who's been a good boy then?*' The dog is probably looking at you and thinking to itself, 'Oh hell, here's that strange person who talks as if he (or she) has a brush handle stuck up their bottom.'

Why can't people talk to their dogs in a normal voice? What is it that makes people do that?

If you now tell me that you didn't recognize yourself within this book, then quite frankly I don't believe you!